Sexual Healing

Praise for Dr. Barbara Keesling's work:

"Finally here is a look at the overwhelmingly positive
effects of sexual expression in our lives, including increased
self-esteem, feelings of personal fulfillment and sexual
ecstasy. Simplify your sex life and breathe some life back
into that divinely sensual body."

— *Whole Life Times*

"In contrast to other how-to books about sex, which often focus
on pleasing your partner at the expense of pleasing yourself,
{Dr. Keesling} presents a series of meditative 'sensate focus'
exercises designed to keep your attention on your own
experience, without wandering off into anxious thoughts about
what your partner might be experiencing. Solidly grounded
in psychological, physiological, and experiential research,
{Dr. Keesling} offers a reassuringly practical approach to
enhancing the quality of sexual experiences."

— *Yoga Journal*

About the Author

Barbara Keesling earned a Ph.D. in Health Psychology from the University of California and taught college courses for many years, lecturing on a variety of psychological topics.

Her books include *Sexual Pleasure, How to Make Love All Night,* and *Talk Sexy to the One You Love.* She has contributed to or been featured in journals including *Redbook, Cosmopolitan, Marie Claire, Healthy Woman, Men's Health, Men's Fitness, GQ Men's Journal, Men's Confidential, Playboy,* and *Bottom Line Personal.* She has appeared on hundreds of television and radio shows, including "Geraldo," "The Montel Williams Show," "Mike and Maty," "The Other Side," "The Howard Stern Show," "Real Personal," and "Gabrielle." Dr. Keesling has been called everything from "The Martha Stewart of Sex" to "the first sex therapist who looks like she's actually had sex!"

SEXUAL HEALING

How Good Loving
is Good for You —
and Your Relationship

Barbara Keesling, Ph.D.

Hunter House
PUBLISHERS

Hunter House Inc., Publishers
P.O. Box 2914
Alameda CA 94501-0914

Library of Congress Cataloging-in-Publication Data
Keesling, Barbara.
Sexual healing : how good loving is good for you and your relationship /
Barbara Keesling.
p. cm.
Includes bibliographical references and index.
ISBN 0-89793-204-8 (pbk.)
1. Sex (Psychology)—Health aspects. 2. Intimacy (Psychology)—Health
aspects. 3. Sex instruction. I. Title.
RA788.K38 1996
615.5—dc 20 96–11480

Project Manager and Editor: Lisa E. Lee   Production Manager: Paul J. Frindt
Copy Editor: Colleen Paretty   Proofreader: Susan Burckhard
Cover Design: MIG Design Works   Book Design: *Qalagraphia*
Marketing & Promotion: Corrine M. Sahli, Kim Wallace
Customer Support: María Jesús Aguiló, Joshua Tabisaura
Publisher: Kiran S. Rana

Printed and Bound by Publishers Press, Salt Lake City, UT
Manufactured in the United States of America

9 8 7 6 5 4 3 2 1   First Edition

Contents

Part Two   Advanced Sexual Healing

List of Exercises

Acknowledgments

I would like to thank everybody at Hunter House, including Kiran Rana, Lisa Lee, Corrie Sahli, Paul Frindt, María Jesús Aguiló, and Josh Tabisaura.

Also, I'd like to thank Michael Riskin, Anita Banker, James Gibbons, Ron Gibb, and all my former therapy colleagues who developed a lot of the exercises in this book.

I would like to thank my clients, because I learned more from you than you ever learned from me.

I would like to thank June Cain Miller—for everything—and besides that, for being a great friend.

This book is dedicated to my clients.

Important Note

The material in this book is intended to provide an overview of sensate focus techniques for improving health through improved arousal, orgasm, and intimacy. Every effort has been made to provide accurate and dependable information. However, you should be aware that professionals in the field may have differing opinions and change is always taking place. Any of the treatments described herein should be used under the guidance of a licensed therapist or health care practitioner. The author, editors, and publisher cannot be held responsible for any outcomes that derive from use of any of these treatments in a program of self-care or under the care of a licensed professional. The treatments in this book should not be used in place of other medical therapies.

*Photograph by
Paul Dahlquist*

Introduction

**F**ive years ago, *David,* a fifty-five-year-old college professor, began to feel fatigued, listless, and weak. He visited his physician for a check-up and had some blood tests run. Within two weeks, he was diagnosed with incurable leukemia. The doctors gave him six weeks to live. As he lay in bed in the intensive care unit, his wife of thirty years sat beside him, massaged his legs, and talked to him as he drifted in and out of consciousness. Today, David is still alive. His body shows no trace of the cancer that almost killed him. He attributes his miraculous recovery to the strong, loving relationship he and his wife have always had. He claims, "She just refused to let me go."

Jay, a thirty-four-year-old stockbroker, suffered from erection problems and rapid ejaculation. As a child he had been sickly, and as an adult he suffered from ulcers and asthma. Jay was single, so when he sought psychological treatment for sexual difficulties, his therapist recommended he work through a series of sensual and sexual exercises with a surrogate partner. The surrogate partner taught Jay breathing and relaxation exercises, in addition to how to have erections and control his ejaculations. Not only did his sexual problems improve, but today he no longer gulps antacids after every meal and has thrown out his inhaler.

Marsha, a forty-year-old divorced, professional woman, visited a chiropractor for chronic back pain that had affected her since her teenage years. The chiropractor's treatment involved manipulating her spine, but he also recommended she get massage. When the male massage professional began working on her lower back, Marsha burst into tears. She suddenly remembered a molestation and attempted rape by her uncle when she was fourteen. Not surprisingly, she had never revealed this event to anyone in twenty-five years—not to her therapist, not to her husband.

Eva, fifty-eight, had always had problems with anger and had visited therapist after therapist to try to uncover the source. Now Eva is in a relationship with a man who has an unusual ability. His unique style of lovemaking calms her down, and as a result her blood pressure has lowered and her migraine headaches are less frequent. She no longer battles the anger she once did.

What do all of these people have in common? All have experienced the magnificent healing power of touch. Some of these stories may seem commonplace, others miraculous, but they all illustrate that touch, in different types of relationships, can be healing. That isn't the end of the story, though. Touching is just the beginning. Research shows that the slow, focused sexual contact that takes place in an intimate, mutual, monogamous relationship—including physical lovemaking up through orgasm—is the most healing touch of all.

You may not have considered lovemaking as a solution to any of your health problems. But it is an aspect of our lives that includes many healing elements: touch, intimacy, communication, physical activity, play, genital activity, arousal, and orgasm. We tend to think of sex as an act. But making love is a creative act, one that involves us on physical, mental, emotional, and spiritual levels. Because lovemaking touches your partner on all these levels at the same time, good love nourishes both of you—and your relationship.

With the information in the next few chapters, you can uncover the "mystery" power that healed David, Marsha, Eva, and Jay and discover your own healing abilities. By exploring and mastering the exercises in this book, you and your partner can act as sexual healers for each other—no small promise in this age of growing conflict and violence between the sexes. You and your partner can learn how to heal yourselves and each other not only sexually, but physically, emotionally, and spiritually as well. In addition to strengthening your intimate connection, you will discover the nuances of mutuality and commitment in your relationship.

The Evolution of Sexual Healing

You may already be familiar with me through my books or as the sex therapist who appears on television, but you may not know about my unusual background. It has given me the unique insights, qualifications, and inspiration to write *Sexual Healing*.

My determination to foster healthy attitudes about sexuality grew out of the dichotomy of growing up in relaxed, sunny Southern California but in a very restrictive, religious family. In 1980, while putting myself through college, I began work as a surrogate partner, assisting people with sexual problems. A surrogate partner is a trained professional who works directly with clients who have sexual problems. In my work I treated clients who had cerebral palsy, multiple sclerosis, and other disabilities that prevented them from working on sexual problems with lovers. I earned a Ph.D. in Health Psychology at the University of California and taught as a college professor for many years.

In 1990, I published my first book, which focused on treating common but psychologically devastating sexual problems, such as the inability to have orgasms, lack of desire, the inability to have erections, premature ejaculation, and inhibited ejaculation. In that first book I adapted typical exercises that surrogate partners do with their clients for use by couples at home.

When I originally wrote that book, I wanted to include chapters on how intimate lovemaking can actually benefit your physical health. I believed then, as I do even more strongly now, that making love can actually improve physical ailments such as ulcers, migraines, and asthma. But at that time there was not enough "scientific" evidence to support these claims—even though I knew they were true from my experiences with clients.

Soon after, I began to read phenomenal stories of spontaneous healing, such as Dr. Paul Pearsall's recovery from cancer, which he describes in his book, *A Healing Intimacy*. Pearsall describes how the power of healing can be generated by committed, long-term, monogamous relationships. I believed it went much deeper than that—sexual healing may occur *best* in that type of relationship, but other relationships that involve touch could be healing also.

Everything jelled when Dr. Pearsall and I were asked to appear on the television show, "The Other Side." (If you are familiar with the show you know that it presented stories on unusual occurrences that are beyond most people's understanding.) The topic of the day was "sexual healing," and we each brought our own perspectives and experiences to bear on the topic. That day it became clear, from the guest and audience reactions, that the time was right to combine our two lines of thinking to show that touch heals, intimacy heals, and the bond created between two people in an intimate, mutual, committed, monogamous sexual relationship is the most healing of all. It is lovemaking in the *deepest* sense of the word. The huge interest generated by this show convinced me that I had unique insights to share and that the time had come to write *Sexual Healing*.

Today, at last, the evidence is clear. Many people have heard stories like those of David, Marsha, Eva, and Jay. Experiences such as theirs happen every day . . . and they can happen to you.

The Dimensions of Sexual Healing

Sexual healing is not just the healing of specifically sexual difficulties. "Sexual healing" encompasses the health-giving, life-affirming effects that sexual arousal and sexual expression can bring to people. Sexual healing uses lovemaking to heal physical ailments, mental difficulties, and emotional problems, as well as promoting healing from the effects of sexual trauma or abuse. It extends to the many ways in which lovemaking can strengthen your immune system, boost your overall health, and deepen your relationship.

In *Sexual Healing* I have tried to convey the holistic, healing powers of loving, sexual contact. Not surprisingly, writing this book has been more difficult than my other books, in part because of the intensely personal nature of this subject and in part because of the unique, intangible powers of sexuality. With this book I hope to inspire people who want something *more* than just a sex manual—people who wish to make love with their hearts, minds, and souls, not simply their bodies.

There are plenty of books out there that can tell you how to boost your immune system or give you tricks for improving your sex life. So, what does *Sexual Healing* do that these books don't? It shows you *how to become a sexual healer.* Unfortunately, when it comes to sex, most people are still stuck wondering whether they are "normal." As a result, current books about sexuality place too much emphasis on orgasm, techniques, and mechanics. And most sex experts offer advice to the tune of "Place Tab A into Slot B." Sadly, our obsessive search for the right partner, the right position, or the right vibrator has blinded us to the joyful, healing aspects of lovemaking.

In *Sexual Healing,* I hope to help you answer questions that are most important to you, questions such as "How do I touch?" "How do I feel better about myself?" and "How do we embrace the spiritual dimension of our relationship?" Because I have had the unique experience of working directly with clients, my books are known for their very practical advice. I offer down-to-earth exercises that really work—and you will find more of these here. The secret door to sexual healing lies in these time-tested exercises, which have helped hundreds of my clients. The exercises will create a physical connection between you and your partner that will open the pathway to emotional and spiritual healing.

The book is divided into two parts—Part One: The Basics of Sexual Healing and Part Two: Advanced Sexual Healing.

The Healing Mindset

In addition to the physical exercises you and your partner do, *Sexual Healing* encourages you to develop a healing mindset. This is the first step to becoming a sexual healer. In anything having to do with health, your expectations and intentions are crucial in determining whether healing will take place. Whenever you do an exercise, take care to gather your energies and attention into a positive, healthful frame of mind. Try to feel the many facets of a loving relationship: unconditional love, acceptance, unselfish good will, complete involvement, positive energy, and lack of pressure or goal orientation. Then, transmit them nonverbally to your partner. Don't expect to be able to feel and convey all of these right away. We are all on a journey toward this mindset. Try, as best you can during any exercise, to embody and convey the expectation that you and your partner will be healed. Over time, after you work with the exercises, you will find that your healing mindset will grow stronger and richer, and will come more naturally.

Intimacy, Mutuality, and Commitment

These qualities are your touchstones, linking the energy of your physical love with the encompassing potential of a healing mindset. To explain these qualities simply: *intimacy* is a feeling of emotional closeness; *mutuality* means experiencing the same thing at the same time or working toward the same goal at the same time; *commitment* is a promise that you agree to keep, whether it is a commitment to stay with your lover, or a commitment to change.

You will find, as you work the exercises, that these qualities both spring from and are necessary to sexual healing. If during one of the exercises you come up against a feeling of resistance, whether a little twinge or something stronger, heed that feeling and consider where it might be coming from. Is it telling you something about the level of intimacy or commitment you and your partner share? Does it illuminate issues within you that need healing? Are you willing to engage in sexual healing exercises, to open up to the powers of mutuality, to tackle these issues?

It's natural to feel hesitant or even a bit intimidated when we realize the power and import of actions we are about to take. But I encourage you to challenge yourself, take the plunge, reach out, and stretch. You will be greatly satisfied by what you find.

If at any time during an exercise you have strong feelings or reactions that you don't feel comfortable pursuing, back off from the exercise and relax with a more basic exercise that gives you comfort, reassurance, and pleasure. Afterward, talk with your partner about what happened and why. Use the opportunity to highlight and address how that aspect needs healing. These sexual healing exercises are for learning, cultivating, and sharing the healing power of intimate sexuality; they are not activities to be "accomplished."

What Is Healing?

I make some extraordinary claims in this book, and I make those claims because I've witnessed extraordinary instances of the power of sexual healing. However, I want to underscore that psychological techniques are no substitute for traditional medical treatments if you need them. The psychological treatments in this book are *adjuncts,* to be used *along with* traditional medicine, not instead of it. When I claim that making love will heal your mind, your body, and your relationship, I mean that you will experience a healthful improvement. You yourself must gauge the degree of that improvement. We are all on a journey toward health, but because no state of perfect "health" exists, your degree of healing will be relative to the place from which you and your partner start.

Who Can Benefit from Sexual Healing?

In general, *Sexual Healing* is for all people who want to make love and feel better! These exercises have been very beneficial for couples who have a strong sexual bond and would like to use that bond to bring strength to or heal other aspects of their relationship. Sexual healing is helpful for people in relationships that no longer include physical lovemaking, and for people of any age with physical conditions that they believe prevent them from making love. People who suffer from specific sexual problems or who were sexually abused have also used these exercises with great success. There are even many exercises for people who don't have partners. I have written *Sexual Healing* with heterosexual couples in mind because that is who I work with most, but these exercises can certainly be used by people of all sexual orientations.

Embarking on the Sexual Healing Journey

Most of the chapters in *Sexual Healing* include exercises you can do at home. Some of these have appeared in different forms in my previous books, but are placed into a new framework and context here. Most exercises are new to this book. Some are for you alone and some are for couples. And don't let the concept of "exercise" scare you away—you don't have to be especially physically fit. These exercises are not strenuous; they involve touch, sensuality, and sexuality. On the other hand, these exercises are not meant simply to improve mechanical prowess; they are entryways to the great powers that come from a deeper appreciation of yourself, your lover, your sexuality, and your relationship.

To use this book to best advantage, read it completely through once. The first few chapters—Chapters 2, 3, 4, and 5—contain basic information and exercises that will develop the sexual healing techniques you need for later, focused healing work. Chapter 1, Which Aspects of Your Life Need Healing?, helps you determine which aspects of your life—physical, mental, spiritual, or relationship aspects—will benefit from sexual healing. Those of you embarking on relationships can learn to create a healing bond between you and your lover right from the outset. Chapter 2, The Healing Touch, explains the fascinating process of how and why sex heals, and how you can use touch to heal both physical and mental problems.

Chapters 3, 4, and 5 teach you the techniques that are basic to all sexual healing exercises. These techniques unlock your healing energies and develop your healing mindset. Chapter 3 has bonding exercises that gently and powerfully lay the emotional foundation on which you and your partner build a sexually healing relationship. These exercises develop a healing resonance in the way you relate to each other. Chapter 4 tackles a different aspect of healing—physical sexual fitness. By gaining a relaxed, masterful sense of your physical abilities you can join them with your emotional and spiritual feelings to make healing sexual unions. In Chapter 5 you will draw on your new-found emotional and physical knowledge to try some beginning sexual healer exercises.

Once you have these basics down, you can decide which issues to work on next: your emotions, your bodies, your relationship, or your spirituality. The second half of the book devotes separate chapters to each of these. Later chapters teach you specific ways to be a sexual healer and to use lovemaking to heal, even if you or your partner has a chronic illness. Chapter 6 introduces peaking and plateauing exercises, which are components of healing sexual intercourse. I also recommend treatments for curing specifically sexual problems and have a special section that discusses how to bring healing power to your relationship with trust and respect, even if you or your partner have experienced sexual abuse. Finally, I have included a chapter on discovering a spiritual element in your lovemaking that will bring you and your partner in contact with something larger than yourself and your relationship.

I recommend the following program: Do the basic breathing, relaxation, and pelvic fitness exercises in Chapters 4 and 5 every day. Then, do one or two of the bonding exercises in Chapter 3 and one or two of the sexual healing exercises in Chapter 5 and beyond once a week. Work through Chapter 6, repeating the peaking and plateauing exercises until you can easily maintain high levels of arousal.

After a few weeks of these exercises, if you don't have a specific sexual problem, move on to Chapters 7 and 8. If you have a physical ailment, continue on to Chapter 9. If you do have a specific sexual problem, don't start Chapter 6 until you have done the appropriate exercises in Chapters 10 and 11. With this pace, you should be able to do most of this program in two to three months, and your health and relationship will begin to show the wonderful effects of it.

Feel free to go back anytime and repeat an exercise if you liked it or if you feel you were anxious and didn't get a lot out of it. Keep in mind that everyone and every couple advances at their own pace. Take the time to feel secure and comfortable with the beginning exercises before you jump into anything more advanced.

Also, make sure that you nourish your emotional and spiritual connection alongside your physical, sexual abilities. If you skip the basics or try to take shortcuts in the advanced exercises, you will be shortchanging yourselves—and your relationship. It takes loving care, focused attention, and gentle perseverance to nurture the healing powers of an intimate relationship.

Part One

The Basics of Sexual Healing

Photograph by Paul Dahlquist

Chapter 1

Which Aspects of Your Life Need Healing?

o you have physical problems that need healing? Or perhaps you suffer from mild anxiety, depression, or other negative emotions. Maybe you are physically and emotionally fit but feel a vague, spiritual unease, a yearning for meaning in your life. Better yet, you are happy with yourself and satisfied in your relationship, and believe that life can be even better. If any of these describe you, you could benefit from sexual healing.

Sexual healing? What do these issues have to do with making love, you may ask. Believe it or not, making love can heal many aspects of your life. Sex is often put down, taken for granted, described as just a physical release, something that animals do, even sinful. But it can become, as Mae West once put it, "an emotion in motion." Making love is an expression, an exchange, an involvement that connects you—whether you like it or not—not only sexually and physically, but mentally, emotionally, and even spiritually with another person. Because lovemaking involves you so completely, it can affect you and your partner in any or all of these areas. In this chapter, we will explore the vast healing potential that lovemaking holds and how it is powered by your mind, body, and soul.

How can healing help if I'm well to begin with? The power of healing, whether it is physical or emotional, is generally positive and healthful. When channeled toward a specific ailment, it has curative effects. When embraced by a healthy person, it brings about greater strength, vitality, and well-being.

As you read about various aspects of sexual healing, consider which will benefit you most and decide how you would like to begin bringing these into your life. The mind and the body affect each other, working together as a system. As a result, you can tap into the system at any point (working on either physical, emotional, sexual, or spiritual problems) and all of you will feel the benefits.

The Physical Benefits of Lovemaking

Do you complain about any of the following: ulcers, migraines, asthma, chronic pain, circulation problems, skin problems, general malaise, lack of physical fitness? Complain no longer, for I have seen lovemaking work wonders on these conditions! When I worked as a surrogate partner, many of my clients had physical conditions such as asthma, ulcers, and other gastrointestinal problems. When they realized healing in sexual areas, their physical conditions improved as well. Chapter 9 details how to heal these specific physical problems, but making love, in general, holds great overall physical benefits.

There are so many healthful perks that it is hard to know where to start. Sex, making love, is a physical process that involves the interplay of many body systems, especially your respiration and blood flow. Since making love stimulates your breathing and increases your oxygen intake, it can increase your lung capacity. When you breathe, oxygen is drawn into your lungs and then absorbed into your bloodstream. Sex both deepens your breathing and increases the oxygen you take in and helps get your blood pumping, which moves that oxygen through your body. When you make love, a great deal of blood flows to your genitals to cause arousal, erection, and lubrication. When you become highly aroused to the point of orgasm, your circulation increases in all areas of the body, especially in your skin and the muscles of your arms and legs. And just like the love songs say, making love makes your heart beat stronger.

Lovemaking is also a well-known analgesic: it relieves pain. When we experience significant arousal or engage in strenuous physical activity, our brain releases chemicals called endorphins. Endorphins, which have been likened to opiates such as morphine or heroin, have painkilling properties and are responsible for altered states of consciousness, such as the "runner's high."

I have found that the best way to get your body producing these fabulous endorphins is to allow your sexual arousal to climb in predictable patterns (see "peaking," in Chapter 6). Then, orgasm triggers a tremendous release of endorphins, which can stop pain for up to several hours. Can you think of a better way to find pain relief? That standard cliché, "Not tonight, dear, I have a headache" should really be the opposite: "Let's make love tonight, honey—I have a headache!" The pain-relieving endorphin effect can work both for short-term pain such as a migraine and chronic pain such as arthritis.

The release of endorphins has an added benefit, aside from pain relief: it boosts your immune system in both the short term and the long term. The endorphin release from arousal and lovemaking encourages relaxation in much the same way as meditation, exercise, and yoga, and this strengthens your immune response. People who have more reliable release of endorphins tend to report fewer symptoms and get sick less. So, sexual touch, arousal, and lovemaking can be a delightful way to help heal painful, immune system-related conditions such as arthritis.

Lovemaking can be very good for relieving physical problems related to reproduction. As many women have discovered, often by accident, making love is exceptionally effective for menstrual difficulties, including painful periods and premenstrual syndrome. Many men with prostate problems experience relief by using the sexual healing techniques for arousal and ejaculation.

Are you worried about your bones? Lovemaking can help ward off osteoporosis because it involves physical exercise. Making love often, whether vigorously or for long periods of time, exercises the long muscles of your arms and legs, and gives your body a more sculpted look. For the same reasons, making love can step up your metabolism and help you lose weight. Lovemaking makes you look and feel better overall: your hair is shinier, your eyes are brighter, and your skin is fresher and radiant—all circulatory benefits.

As wonderful as lovemaking is, there are some things that it cannot do for your health. It can't make up for horrible health habits such as eating junk food, smoking, taking drugs, or using alcohol excessively. But with all the good feelings that come from sexually inspired health, you may find yourself drawn to healthier habits anyway.

The Psychological Benefits of Lovemaking

Are you already in good physical shape? Then you can enjoy the physical well-being that sexual healing inspires and focus on bringing healing to other areas of your life. Our emotions color the fabric of our sexual life. They provide the context in which we make love—or abstain from it. What most people don't realize is that the way in which we make love can nourish our emotional state. Depression and anxiety are the two most common emotional issues that affect our sex life and that can be positively affected by lovemaking. I'll address them specifically, because they are the root of many sexual problems and deep unfulfillment.

Depression refers to a general feeling of misery or sadness that usually includes loss of appetite, loss of sex drive, excessive sleep, and general feelings of worthlessness. Depression can also result in complete loss of interest in life and lack of motivation. If you are feeling depressed, you can learn how to become aroused and restore that joie de vivre by following the steps outlined in Chapter 6.

Anxiety is a more complicated issue, and is also strongly related to sexuality. The physical symptoms of anxiety include sweating, muscle tension, shortness of breath, cold hands and feet, and rapid heart rate. Mental symptoms of anxiety include worrying, obsessing, and an inability to relax. These symptoms, both physical and mental, directly affect your ability to experience arousal, feel sexual pleasure, and enter an intimate, loving sphere. Because anxiety can cause severe sexual problems, understanding what causes it is the key to halting it.

Your Body's Two Nervous Systems

Our nervous system has two separate and complementary subsystems. One of these, the sympathetic nervous system or SNS, is responsible for speeding up your physical responses. This is the system that delivers the so-called "fight or flight" response. It mobilizes the energy in your body so that you can run away or otherwise deal with a threatening event. When this system is active, you experience a combination of physical signs: Your heart beats rapidly, your eyes dilate, you perspire, and blood rushes away from the center of your body to your limbs. You also experience psychological signs, especially anxiety.

The other subsystem, the parasympathetic nervous system or PNS, is just the opposite. It is active when your body takes care of its life-sustaining processes, such as regulating heartbeat and digestion. It slows your body down so that you conserve energy. As a result, we experience this system's activity as relaxation.

So what is the tie-in to sexual healing, you ask? The two nervous systems generally cannot be active at the same time; we know this because it is difficult to be relaxed when we are anxious or aroused. But to make satisfying, healing love, you must cultivate sensual arousal while consciously engaging your relaxation nervous system. The pleasure of the arousal and the relaxation of engaging your parasympathetic nervous system will do wonders to relieve anxiety and flood you with well-being.

How do I know so much about anxiety? I've treated hundreds of patients with the problem. Taking patients who suffer from panic disorder (not general anxiety but a very severe, clinical form of anxiety) and teaching them to relax and make love is one of my specialties. In addition to professional expertise, I would venture that another reason I have been helpful to anxious people is that I have experienced anxiety for most of my life. (I jokingly refer to myself as "the anxiety-disorder spokesperson.") I have learned and put into practice all these exercises myself, to keep from being paralyzed with anxiety.

It is possible to have both anxiety and depression at the same time—isn't life wonderful? And since our minds and bodies are so intimately connected, if you have anxiety or depression, you probably experience some physical problems too. A lot of research shows that people who have chronic negative emotions such as anxiety and depression are also likely to have heart problems, migraines, ulcers, asthma, and arthritis. (Incidentally, much of this research was done by my Ph.D. adviser, Dr. Howard Friedman, at the University of California. If you are interested in reading more about this, pick up a copy of his book, *The Self-Healing Personality*).

If you have mild to moderate depression or anxiety, you can use the sexual healing program to lift your state of mind. If you have severe problems with either, please consult a mental health professional as well.

Other Emotional and Mental Benefits

Would you like to have a better body image or stronger self-esteem? Perhaps you feel emotionally solid, but wish to improve your mental faculties. Would you like to increase your concentration or memory? Maybe you suffer from boredom, and you want to recharge your inspiration? Perhaps you have a problem, such as post-traumatic stress disorder, or wish to get past other toxic emotions or attitudes such as hostility or negativity. Do you occasionally experience insomnia, fatigue, or chronic stress? If so, you will benefit from introducing the healing power of lovemaking into your life.

Mentally, making love can have other benefits. It can inspire your imagination and increase your sensitivity. The sexual healing exercises teach you to channel your thoughts and energies in directions that you wish, thus multiplying their force. By releasing oxytocin, that wonderful hormone you may have read about in the news, lovemaking can boost your creativity, heighten your senses. Oxytocin may also help concentration, mental acuity, and focus.

Making love will make you less self-conscious and less concerned about what other people think about you. Many of the exercises in this book will raise your self-esteem by showing you that your partner finds your body—and you—desirable. You thus become active and instrumental in gaining what you desire instead of waiting passively for good feelings to come to you.

Lovemaking can also build self-esteem through a more complex mechanism. Research shows sexuality is tied closely to personality, and self-esteem is a *huge* part of your personality. I do not mean that you can't feel good about yourself if you don't make love with another person—of course you can. But I do not believe it is possible to feel good about yourself unless you *accept* your sexual feelings and *accept* your decisions about whether to act on those feelings or not. So sexuality can be a source of self-esteem even if you choose not to make love with another person. The sexual healing program in this book will build your self-esteem by helping you learn this self-acceptance.

I have tried to show you how sexual healing will work for you and your partner. But you may be surprised to know it can also work for society in general. Lovemaking can help you get rid of performance orientation and competitive striving, behaviors that help us to be productive in work and play but are destructive in relationships. Lovemaking (especially the techniques described in Chapters 5, 6, 7, and 8), can increase your empathy—your ability to feel what another person is feeling—because it can hone your ability to read another person's nonverbal cues.

Lovemaking can also give you the energy to help others. Because it increases your sex drive or libido, it also increases your life drive, your *elan vital,* your *joie de vivre.* Because you will experience this healing energy and want to share it with others, making love could actually improve your character and make you a better person!

How Lovemaking Heals Your Emotions

Our sexual drive differs from other basic biological drives, such as hunger and thirst. While we can't live without food or water, we can physically survive without making love or reproducing. I say "physically survive" because I don't believe we are really living when this drive goes unfulfilled. Part of us, our sexual and emotional self, atrophies when it is not acknowledged.

Sexual expression may also contribute to your health in an indirect way. For example, sexual contact can provide a buffer against stress. Lovemaking is one form of what psychologists call "social support"—the human contact that people have available to them or that they believe is available to them. Having a person with whom you can self-disclose, a person you can openly express feelings to and discuss them with, is one of the most valuable forms of social support. A satisfying, lovemaking relationship creates an excellent atmosphere in which to express feelings.

The Mind-Body Relationship

The mind-body problem is one that has occupied philosophers and psychologists for hundreds of years, so I am not likely to resolve it here. However, the reason lovemaking can heal your body and your mind is because of this relationship. Our minds affect our bodies, and our bodies affect our minds. (Some of the ways this exchange works was the subject of a wonderful series Bill Moyers did with PBS, called "Healing and the Mind.")

Most people are familiar with the concept of psychosomatic illness—the idea that our attitudes and emotions can influence whether or not we get sick and how quickly we get better, and even affect the development of chronic health problems such as heart disease and cancer. The idea that an illness is psychosomatic does not mean that it is all in one's head or is not real. It means that our psyche plays some part in it, no matter how small. In a sense all medical problems are psychosomatic, because being sick affects us psychologically. The fact that our mind can influence our body has made it possible to design treatments, such as relaxation and visualization, for cancer and chronic illnesses.

Sigmund Freud was the first to examine psychosomatic illness and its connection to sexuality. Freud thought that repressed sexual conflicts could emerge as physical symptoms, and he seems to have been right. If sexual interactions are a source of conflict or anxiety for you, they may also be negatively affecting your physical health. Many people intuitively recognize that their sexual interactions cause them stress, and attempt to remedy the situation by avoiding sex. Unfortunately, denying the problem will not make it go away, so these people find that even if they give up sexual activities, their ailments remain. Sometimes they worsen. Their complaints may take on a different physical form but they don't just go away, because the lack of sexual activity becomes a source of unconscious conflict.

If you harbor a fear of sexuality that may be causing health problems, the exercises in this book will give you a way to relearn sexual expression in a gradual and nonthreatening manner. You can then use this positive sexual experience as a way to heal your body, your mind, and your relationship.

Let me caution you that the relationship between sexuality and health has not been scientifically "proven" by psychologists—researchers only know that these things seem to be related to each other in predictable ways. I would like to be able to say definitively that improving your sex life will improve your overall physical and mental health and well-being, because in my experience this is true. But, believe it or not, no psychologist or scientist has ever tried to research this question! So, we have no formal, scientific studies showing that pleasurable sexual activity keeps you healthy or that lack of sexual expression causes illness.

Healing Specific Sexual Issues

Because sexuality is such an intimate area of our lives and hits at the core of who we are, we may be reluctant to seek help for the problems that arise in our bedrooms. For those of you who are seeking specific sexual help, I have included chapters on how to heal men's and women's sexual difficulties. For men, these include low desire, problems with erections, inability to become aroused or have an orgasm, and premature ejaculation. For women, these issues include low desire, inability to become aroused or have an orgasm, and sexual pain disorders such as vaginismus and dyspareunia. These problems can be turned around, and with some patience and a loving touch, they will be.

Enhancing Relationships

We naturally think of making love as an expression of our *relationship*, but we may not appreciate how it can be a vital and dynamic process of our actual *relating*. There are many ways that lovemaking can strengthen or heal your relationship that are not obvious.

When we come to lovemaking with conscious intention, we open ourselves to the ways in which it can affect us, instead of limiting sexual experiences to what our emotional and mental states project. Making passionate, intimate love lowers your psychological defenses and helps you become more vulnerable. And making love sets the stage for you to share feelings; there is something about being naked together and intimately caressing bodies that inspires couples to share feelings and tell the truth. This kind of intimacy engenders trust and brings deeper knowledge of yourself and your partner. Lovemaking uncovers the facets of your commitment. It can increase your generosity and reinforce the give-and-take present in healthy relationships. Lovemaking is a beautiful, effortless way to communicate feelings in situations where words get in the way or just don't express what you need to say to your partner.

Deepening Spirituality

Are you working on strengthening the more intangible aspects of yourself? Do you experience needs of a spiritual or even existential nature? Many of us are searching for a deeper meaning in life, a connection to something larger than ourselves. At the core, these are spiritual issues. Our spiritual understanding informs all aspects of our lives, holistically, but we catch glimpses of spiritual insight more easily when we are focused on specific areas of our life.

If you are reasonably fit, happy in your relationship, mentally active, sexually satisfied, and emotionally healthy but still looking for that intangible "something" that you sense is missing, try sexual healing. Chapter 13 offers specific techniques for awakening your sexual spirit.

Are there any other benefits to lovemaking that I might have missed? Probably. Making love is a rare experience reinvented and made new each time a couple comes together. You may feel I've made lovemaking sound as if it is the greatest thing on earth . . . I believe that it is. While it may never put a person on the moon, it certainly brings a celestial joy to our lives.

A Word about Safe Sex

No book on sexuality is complete without a mention of safe sex. And safety, when it comes to sexuality, can mean a couple of things.

First, even though lovemaking is so wonderful, sex can be used for inappropriate purposes. If your sex life involves nonconsensual partners, coercion, abuse, or compulsion, or partners under the legal age, I urge you to address these issues immediately and get help to change them. The sexual healing program can help you, within the bounds of appropriate, healthful sexual expression, and I suggest paying special attention to Chapter 12.

Second, *Sexual Healing* has been written primarily for couples in a committed, monogamous, long-term relationship, because I believe that kind of loving is the setting in which the most powerful healing can take place. However, I recognize that you may be in the beginning stages of a relationship, or that you may wish to use some of the exercises outside of a monogamous relationship.

While I prefer to focus on the positive aspects of making love, the reality of life today is that there are risks. If you are in the beginning stages of a relationship, if you are not sure of your partner's past, if you have multiple partners, or if you engage in high-risk behavior, please use condoms during any activities in which there is any exchange of body fluids. If you use condoms, make sure the lubrication you use is water-based, since oils can and will cause condoms to break. If your relationship and your commitment deepens, consider getting tested to ensure you are both free from sexual disease. Once those issues are resolved, you will feel safer and freer to make love without condoms.

Photograph by
Charlotte Morrison

Chapter 2

The Healing Touch

he essence of touch begins within our skin. We may not realize it, but many of us need to heal some aspect of our relationship with our own body. Beginning in childhood, society bombards us with unrealistic messages about what our body is and what it should be. At the very least we grow up detached from our bodies, viewing them as garments or tools. Sexual healing reconnects our mind and body and uses the power of that unity for our health and well-being. If whole body health is what we are after, how our body *feels* is more important than what it *does* and how it *looks*. The key to knowing our body's feelings lies in the simple ability to give and receive touch.

Touch Is Vital

Touching has been a traditional treatment for illness throughout human history. In religious history, figures such as Jesus and some saints used laying on of hands to heal people. Later, in Europe, those who were ill and infirm were brought before the king, whose touch would supposedly cure them. Today, *curanderas* in Mexican and Latin American communities often use touch as part of their treatments.

Touch can communicate a number of things, such as comfort and positive expectations. As a result, touch influences our physical well-being. In fact, there is quite a bit of research on the positive health effects of touch. Much of it has been brought together by

Ashley Montagu in his classic book, *Touching* (1986). Montagu describes how skin contact affects mental and physical health throughout all stages of our lives, beginning with birth. Studies show that infants who are touched have much higher survival rates than those who are deprived of human contact. Infants who are stroked and caressed develop more healthily, and later in life they develop fewer clinical emotional and mental problems. Other studies with adults find that being touched can lower heart rate and blood pressure and promote physical relaxation in general. Even simply stroking a pet can lower blood pressure and heart rate.

There is no doubt that infants and children need touch to survive, and although there is no research on whether adults *need* touch, there is also no reason to believe that our need to be touched ends with childhood. The countless good ways that touch benefits us—heals us—may be the reason we feel so good when touched. While I hope this book introduces you to the wonders of sexual healing, I believe the greatest thing it will do is deepen your appreciation for the magic of all touch.

The Nonverbal Power of Touch

In the language of nonverbal communication, touch is an "intensifier." This means that whatever mood already exists in a given situation, touch will make that mood stronger. Remember the first time your partner reached out to touch you before you became lovers? Or, when you were a little child and bumped your head, having your mother hold you and hug you made the pain go away much faster than if she said, "There, there . . . now go and play."

Not all touch intensifies good feelings. Here is a common example: Let's say you have just met someone and on first impression, for whatever reason, this person gives you the creeps. If this person touches you while you are talking, your mood toward him or her will become even more negative.

Touch also conveys power, particularly in the workplace. If an employer touches a subordinate during an interaction, this intensifies their awareness of the difference in power between them. Whether consciously or not, many people use touch to communicate their feelings and intentions.

In *Sexual Healing* you will learn to use the intensifying power of touch for positive purposes, to bring healing energy to your mind, body, and intimate relationships. If a healing attitude already exists between you and your partner, touching will intensify the healing intent you two already exchange.

The Healing Powers of Touch

Touch has been shown to have various, positive healing effects. I believe this is because touch addresses both your body and your mind. For example, touching may have a positive effect on the immune system. Ashley Montagu describes research on rats, which shows that rats that are handled when they are young have better-developed immune systems as adults.

Touching also makes it easier to share feelings. Studies show that touch encourages self-disclosure. For example, patients touched in the genital region by doctors and nurses during a physical examination often reveal personal sexual information. It appears that being touched in intimate areas taps into intimate thoughts and feelings.

Not surprisingly, touch has positive effects on people facing medical recovery. For example, patients touched by nurses recover faster than those who are not touched. It is not known precisely how touching in this situation helps people get better. It could be that touch directly promotes relaxation, that it stimulates our pain-killing and healing mechanisms. Or, it could be that the act of touching communicates care, and imparts to the patient a sense of self-worth and the expectation of becoming well. I suspect it is a combination of these things.

The Touch that Heals

A sexual, intimate relationship offers an excellent context in which we can experience the healing powers of touch. Sadly, the social norms for adults in North American culture do not encourage or allow much physical contact. For many of us, especially men, sexual encounters are the only situations in which we actively touch other human beings and enjoy being touched by them. Just loosening our cultural inhibition against hugging could probably do more for our health than half the diet and fitness programs in the United States.

There is a particular kind of touch—and way to touch—that is healing. For sexual healing to occur, you will need to develop a healing intention, described in Chapter 1, so that you nonverbally convey your healing expectation. You will also need to learn the specific way to touch that induces healing.

This type of healing touch is called *sensate focus*. The term sensate focus may sound technical but it is actually quite simple—and self-explanatory. It is a technique in which you focus your attention as closely as you can on your sensations. This is the essence of the sexual healing exercises: direct all your attention—and intention—on where you touch your skin, or your partner's skin, and where your partner touches you. If your mind wanders off during an exercise, consciously bring it back to the place of your connection and what you are experiencing.

The touch that heals is called a *caress*. It is a delicate touch to the skin, not a massage or pressure. A healing caress has the following characteristics:

- *It is very slow.* As you caress in these exercises, practice slowing the speed at which you touch by half.

- *It is pressure-free.* There should be no pressure to perform sexually, either on yourself or on your partner.

- *It is focused.* You pay attention to the temperature, texture, contrast, and shape of what you touch. If you become distracted at any point, consciously bring your mind back to where you are touching or being touched.

- *It is in the here and now.* As you touch, if you start thinking about the past or the future, bring yourself back to what you feel now.

- *It is sensuous.* As you touch, experience the pure pleasure of your skin or your partner's skin.

The three exercises in this chapter set the stage for the healing techniques you will learn in the rest of the book. They teach how to touch something else to relax, and how to touch yourself in a relaxing, healing way.

♀ Exercise ♂
Touching an Inanimate Object

In this first exercise, you will touch an inanimate object. This introduces you to sensate focus touch and prepares you to work first with yourself and later with a partner. It may seem a little silly at first, but I have asked you to begin with an object, not your lover, so that you are not self-conscious. By the time you do come together with your partner, touching in this healing way will be second nature.

Before You Begin Set aside about fifteen minutes during which you will not be disturbed. Pick some things to touch (two or three things) that look like they would feel good, a piece of velvet or a fur rug, for example.

The Exercise Place a good thing to touch on your lap (let's say it is the velvet). Lightly touch it with rhythmic strokes, as slowly as you can. Focus all your attention on how your fingers feel on that velvet. Close your eyes. Don't think about what just happened or what is to come; simply be in the present.

Caress in as many ways as you can think to touch—stroking with the nap, against the nap, up and down, in a circular motion, etc. If your mind drifts, bring it back to what you are doing. Get in touch with sensuality—how this object feels good against your skin.

You cannot caress too slowly. If you think you are moving your hand slowly enough, try cutting your speed in half and see how this affects your ability to focus on the touch.

Stop the exercise after fifteen minutes. Can you feel how relaxed you became from this simple act of touching? Your breathing has slowed, and your heart rate has slowed. This simple touching exercise has the same effect as meditation.

Variation   Instead of something soft like velvet or fur, you could try touching an object that is cold and hard, such as a small statue. I used to keep a small marble statue of a seal for clients to use. It was smooth, with a cool temperature that was pleasing to the touch, and it had lots of curves. Everyone who picked up this statue ended up naturally caressing their face with it because the cool temperature and smooth texture felt so good.

♀ Exercise ♂
Touching Yourself

To learn how you would like to be touched, and in preparation for the sensual exercises you will do later with your partner, it is important to practice sensate focus caresses on yourself. Remember that the emphasis is sensual rather than sexual. By learning to touch yourself in a relaxing, gentle way, you will lay the foundation for all the exercises that follow.

Do you feel a little self-conscious caressing yourself? Many people do, especially when they move to their genitals and especially if they have never touched themselves in this way. This feeling is natural. Practicing the self-caress will make you more comfortable.

It is very important to learn about your own body response so that you can increase your ability to become aroused and awaken your ability to heal yourself and your partner. Of course, as with any exercise, don't do anything you are uncomfortable with.

The Exercise　Choose a setting where you will not be disturbed. Pick a small area of your body, such as your arm, your chest, or your thigh, for your first self-caress. Put some lotion or massage oil on your fingertips and slowly begin to touch yourself.

Focus on the exact point of contact between your hand and your body. If your mind wanders off to something else, bring it back to exactly how your skin feels, both your fingertips and the skin being touched. Stroke yourself slowly and lightly. Touch only the skin; do not massage any muscles. Is your touch sensitive enough to feel your individual hairs? Think about what you feel right now, rather than anything you have been taught or remember from the past.

If you have trouble concentrating, slow down your touch. Use more lotion if your skin feels rough or dry. Spend fifteen minutes doing this, learning the feeling of your hand against your skin.

♀ Exercise ♂
Touching Your Genitals

In this exercise you will caress your genital area, but this touch is not the same as masturbation. Many adults use masturbation as a comforting way to receive touch, but the genital caress is somewhat different. The goal is not to feel sexual, turn yourself on, or have an orgasm. The goal is to learn what kind of touch you like. What feels good? If you do this exercise with the healing attitude we talked about in the introduction, you will also learn that it is healthy—not selfish—to touch yourself.

Before You Begin   Sit or lie naked in a comfortable position, in a comfortable space. Remember that caressing is not the same as masturbating. The purpose of this exercise is not to have an orgasm but to learn the different, pleasurable sensations of your body.

The Exercise for Women   Warm some baby oil or other lubricant on your fingers and begin to slowly touch your inner thighs and your vaginal lips. If any part of your body feels tense, make a conscious effort to relax it. This caress may include only your outer genitalia or you can stroke inside your vagina as well. Do whatever you are comfortable with and will enjoy.

Concentrate on the touch exactly the way you did when you caressed the other part of your body in the previous exercise. If your mind starts to wander off, slow down the movement of your hand and consciously bring your mind back to that point where skin touches skin.

Try different touches. Touch yourself the way your partner usually touches you, then the way you usually touch yourself, then in a completely different way. Caress your outer and inner lips, your clitoris, and the opening to your vagina. Do not spend any more time on your clitoris than you do on other parts of your genitals. Relax all your muscles and keep your breathing even. Concentrate on the landscape of your body—the changes in texture, temperature, and arousal as you touch different areas.

If you become sexually aroused, that is perfectly okay, but remember that it is not the goal. The only goals are to enjoy yourself and to learn about your own body. If you become aroused, make a conscious effort to relax your muscles and take a deep breath. Gently, slowly stroke yourself to feel maximum sensual awareness and sensual enjoyment.

If you have an orgasm, that is okay. Do not try to make it happen, do not try to make it better or stronger, and do not try to push it away. Try not to tense up against it; just experience it. Continue caressing for about fifteen minutes.

The Exercise for Men　　Use some baby oil or lotion on your fingers if you like. Slowly begin to caress your penis and scrotum, concentrating on the temperature and texture of your skin. Don't worry about whether you have an erection—you don't need one to do the exercise. You are just exploring the sensations your penis and scrotum are capable of and which types of touch feel good.

Keep your attention on the exact point of contact between your fingers and your genitals. If your mind wanders off, slow the movement of your hand and bring your mind back to the touch. Experiment with different types of touch. Touch yourself the way you usually do, the way your partner does, and in as many different ways you can think of.

Keep all the muscles in your body relaxed and breathe evenly. If you feel yourself approaching orgasm, that is okay. Don't push to make it happen, try to make it better, or push it away. Just allow orgasm to come to you. Continue caressing for fifteen minutes.

———————————

Congratulations! You've taken the first step toward sexual healing. Pretty easy, huh? After completing these exercises, most people experience a heightened awareness. A lot of people feel better about themselves immediately. Still others see themselves as more sensual and sexual. A few people have very intense experiences with these exercises—the genital caress may bring up feelings of sadness or tearfulness, but this is part of the sexual healing process.

Lawrence found the exercise Touching an Inanimate Object "calming, almost like meditation." After the Touching Yourself exercise, *Jeanne* said, "I felt better about myself immediately. I started to accept my body for how it felt instead of how it looked." What feelings about yourself and your body came up for you?

Feel free to explore these exercises further, or move on to the next chapter. In it you will find basic steps for healing your relationship.

A Note about Harmful Touch

Not all sexual touch is healing. Sexual touch can be used coercively, especially inappropriate sexual touch between adults and children. This kind of touch is highly destructive: it betrays intimacy and trust; it exploits power dynamics. Sexual molestation and abuse are especially sad because they pervert something good. People who experience this childhood abuse often have difficulty with sexual touch later in life.

Photograph by
Paul Dahlquist

Chapter 3

Setting the Stage for
a Healing Relationship

s a sex therapist who has written several self-help books, I appear frequently on television to discuss sexual issues. In many cases, the hosts open the show up to questions from a studio audience or people calling in from home. The question I am most frequently asked is some version of, "How do I put the spark, the passion, back in my love life?"

A Crisis of Intimacy

It is clear that a lot of people have decent relationships—they are physically healthy, their kids are okay, and they get along well, but many feel they have lost their sexual desire, their passion and joy. A few couples have more serious problems; their relationship may be a setting for conflict or even violence. This book offers solutions to increase intimacy if you have been together for a number of years and that spark is sputtering. You will also find advice on healing your relationship if it has been marred by abuse either in the distant or recent past.

In this chapter, however, I'd like to concentrate on how to build intimacy, mutuality, commitment, and healing into your relationship if you are just starting out together. If you've been in a relationship for a while, don't despair! You can still use the exercises in this chapter to get to know each other again—a lot of times, healing your relationship means having a chance to start over.

Choosing the Right Partner

Are you embarking on a relationship and wondering whether the relationship has the capacity for a lifetime of sexual healing? The first thing to keep in mind, obviously, is choosing the right partner. How do you distinguish a potential intimate partner for life from one who will bail at the first sign of trouble?

First, there are some things to look for, warning signs that this is *not* the right person. These include physical, verbal, or emotional abuse; manipulation; dishonesty; criticism; and, especially, violence. Does this relationship make you anxious and depressed? Does your partner manipulate you by alternately clinging with dependency, then withdrawing? If you have not made a commitment to this relationship, it is best to get out now. (If you have made a commitment to this relationship, see Chapter 12.)

Most of the warning signs are obvious, and if you are not invested in the relationship it can be headed off at this point. But what do you look for beyond this? Most people start relationships for the wrong reasons: they are emotionally needy or vulnerable and they like a person's looks, are attracted to them chemically, or like a particular aspect of the other's personality, such as sense of humor. Unfortunately, none of these qualities really predicts continued growth of intimacy over the years. It sounds old-fashioned, but you have to look at the qualities that *have* been shown to lead to increased intimacy and longevity of the relationship—qualities like character and values.

It is very difficult to judge another person's character, especially if you are young and just starting out in a relationship. First off, your assessment has to be age-appropriate. For example, you wouldn't expect a twenty-year-old to be running a corporation. However, you *could* look at how that twenty-year-old treats and talks about his or her parents, siblings, friends, and strangers; you could find out about the way he or she approaches life and loved ones. If I wanted to start a relationship with an older person who had a lot more life experience, I would also want to know not *what* they have achieved but *why*. Who is a better relationship bet if your goal is lifelong intimacy, mutuality, and commitment: someone who refers to his ex-wife as "a shrew" or someone who makes an effort to get along with an ex-spouse so the kids have a stable life? Someone who works her way through college and gets good grades, or someone who skips classes right and left because someone else is paying for it?

What Happens When Boy Meets Girl?

Some of us are able to navigate the treacherous waters of romance and find a decent partner. But a lot of us are picking partners using the wrong criteria (looks, money, status, and so forth), and too many others are choosing partners too early.

Let's look at the dynamics that typically occur with young couples. The following scenario is typical of couples I see in therapy. *Melissa* and *David* began dating in their late teens or early twenties. Aside from a few dalliances, neither is really sexually experienced. Both live with their parents. They date for all the "right" reasons: they are similar in looks and personality, and appear to have a lot in common. At some point, David pressures Melissa into having sex, and they have it when they can—often in his car. They don't have foreplay, and sex is over before it really starts. Melissa doesn't really enjoy the sex, although it gets somewhat better as their relationship progresses, but she feels they have become closer.

When the two reach a certain age, they experience a lot of social pressure to marry. They do, and they have two children. Within a few years of marriage they find themselves stressed out. Work, school, and the kids have taken priority over time alone and lovemaking. Out of boredom, isolation, or alienation, one or both have an affair, and they think sex with their new lover is the greatest they've ever had. When they divorce, everyone says, "What a shame. They must have grown apart."

But guess what? They were never together. Melissa and David's relationship reached a peak of intimacy when they were still dating, at about the time right before they had sex. That was the point at which they felt closest to each other. They may have reached another moment of intimacy when they had their first child. But as they went about their day-to-day lives, they missed communicating, sharing, and growing together, so their relationship became less intimate over time instead of more intimate. So, what went wrong, you ask?

What didn't go wrong? Neither David nor Melissa knew anything about their own body or how to relate sexually and intimately to a lover. It is not a matter of whether they had sex too early in the relationship or whether they were too young when they first had sex (only they can say). The problem was that they never let intimacy develop—slowly and solidly—between them. And their intimacy did not grow along with their lovemaking.

But who knows how to make intimacy grow? It's not a skill we are taught. Lovemaking is the one area of life in which we are expected to be competent but no one ever tells or shows us how, and we never get to see people do it. The best (or worst) example most of us have is our parents' relationship.

Let's look at another typical scenario. *Joan* and *Richard* meet through work. Joan has a great deal more sexual experience than Richard. She is self-confident, comfortable, and has reached levels of intimacy with past lovers. Richard is anxious about sexual "performance" and loses his erection the first few times they make love. He feels like a failure because he equates lovemaking with erections and penetration. Richard begins to want sex to be quick and furious, to relieve his anxiety—and to convince himself he is sexually okay. Joan and Richard don't have time to reach intimacy in their lovemaking. Again, their relationship progresses; they marry and have children. Although everything else in the relationship is good, the sex is always pretty lousy. Eventually they feel a lack of desire; they feel bored and unsatisfied. These feelings permeate other aspects of their relationship, and Joan and David divorce.

Why do I sound as if I've heard this same story a million times? Because I have. This is *the* typical scenario that people relate when, instead of divorcing, they come in for sex therapy. I teach them how to cultivate sexual healing to solve their sexual problems and to deepen the intimacy and mutuality in their relationship. Most people want to know, "What do you do after the love is gone?" but the question really should be, "What do you do after the hormones are gone?"

In all of these scenarios, the couples reached a level of sexual intimacy much too early in the relationship and lost it steadily thereafter. They expected that the sexual charge they achieved when first dating (when the hormones were really flowing) would and should be the norm for sex throughout their lives. It won't. It can't. People grow and change, and so does their sexual expression.

The good news is that this growth can bring you and your lover closer together. Your relationship *can* improve, and you *can* experience deeper and richer passion as you grow older together— if you work toward it by building intimacy and mutuality.

But I'm not a Joan or Melissa or Richard or David, you say? Of course not; not everybody fits into the situations described above. Unfortunately, this book can't hold detailed explorations of every potential cause for an intimacy crisis. However, as a counterpoint to the couples above, let's look at my own struggle for intimacy. Most people fall somewhere in between my experience and more typical experiences like those above.

Much of my life I have been mistrustful of people who sought to be emotionally close too fast. I attribute this to growing up in a family that was emotionally repressed, in an atmosphere without emotional connection. I came of age in the 1970s, when young people felt "liberated" and had sex partly because they enjoyed it and partly to prove that you didn't have to be "in love" to do it. Not only did I have sex with people I didn't love, to be honest, I had sex with people I would probably cross the street to avoid these days! Then, I wondered why life felt so empty and meaningless.

When I started work as a surrogate, these feelings improved somewhat because, as you will read in Chapter 5, the surrogate-client relationship develops in intimacy at a slower, more healthy pace. It progresses through stages of talking, disclosure, and nonsexual touch before sexual touch begins. This getting comfortable and relaxed before having sex and having nonpressured, nonsexual touch was very different from the "liberated sex" that was espoused in the late '60s and the '70s. Doing surrogate work actually helped heal me from the effects of meaningless, impersonal sex. It allowed me to open up to loving, intimate partnerships.

New Relationships

The most important thing you can do when embarking on a new relationship is to make sure you get intimate with the right person, for the right reasons. Be honest and true to yourself above all else. Is this someone you like and respect? Are you friends? Do you feel this relationship will be dynamic? If so, progress in your conversation and involvement to increasingly more intimate areas.

Keep in mind that both verbal and physical intimacy occur at several levels. When people first meet socially they talk about their tastes—their likes and dislikes, such as movies or music. Unfortunately, most people halt the level of intimate conversation right there. But relationships that last through the years are based on deeper sharing, caring, and understanding. A deeper level of intimacy is to share opinions on value-driven areas such as politics and religion. An even more intimate level is to share emotionally charged material about self-image. The highest level of verbal intimacy includes feelings about sex, possibly including guilt, shame, or inadequacies.

Physical intimacy also progresses in stages. I think of these stages as: sharing something physical together such as a sport; the nonsexual touching that goes on between friends (such as a hug or a peck on the cheek); sexual touch; intercourse; and orgasm. It is truly rare and wonderful when you can share all these levels of physical intimacy with one person. But all in one night? Or one week? You are probably doing some wishful thinking and moving too fast.

If you are just starting out in a relationship and you want the emotional closeness to continue to grow throughout your relationship, make sure that there is always some aspect of lovemaking that you have yet to try. If you and your lover take the time and space necessary for emotional intimacy, you will find that vistas of unexplored sexual expression will unfold for you.

Intimate Bonding

The exercises in this chapter create and strengthen emotional bonds between lovers. "Bonding" usually refers to the emotional connection that develops between a child and his or her caregiving parent. Parents create this vital, intimate bond by spending lots of time together holding, cuddling, hugging, and playing with their child. Sharing those activities gives the child the love, security, and self-worth necessary to venture out into the world and mature fully.

As adults we can bond with each other, too. The following exercises create and strengthen those intimate bonding feelings. But I warn you—don't try these exercises with your partner unless you are sure you want to feel closer. They will help you become relaxed with each other, and attuned to your heart rhythms. They express how you accept your partner and help you feel accepted. It is easy to tell your partner, "I love and accept you," but that does not have the profound impact that holding, stroking, and physically calming your loved one has.

Many couples begin their relationship with a lot of touching and nonsexual contact, but for many this contact stops after awhile. Once their couplehood is established, their touch becomes limited to sexual contact. If there is one complaint I have heard over and over, it is "Whenever he (she) touches me it always leads to sex." If touch becomes one-dimensional, or limited to a particular context, it affects the emotional tenor of the relationship.

Many skeptics feel that an "exercise" for emotional intimacy is a gimmick, that intimacy just naturally happens with physical closeness over time, and that you can't do anything to force it or improve it. I disagree. These exercises are not gimmicks if they are done from the heart, with honest openness, and without manipulative intent. An emotional bond cannot be forced, but it can be given the opportunity to grow. These exercises provide a nonsexual, nonverbal space for intimate feelings to grow, be recognized, and be shared with each other. They start from your existing intimacy and, with the poetic nature of nonverbal communication, they deepen it.

♀ Exercise ♂
Spoon Breathing

The first bonding exercise we will talk about is spoon breathing. Lie together on a comfortable bed or couch with one person's back snuggled up against the other person's front. You and your partner may already naturally fall into some form of this embrace—a lot of couples do—but don't wait for it to happen spontaneously. It's okay to ask your partner, "Can we spoon for a while?"

The Exercise　Lie on your sides with your legs bent so that you fit together like two spoons in a drawer. The person who is in back places his or her hand on the stomach of the person in front. Lie perfectly still and try not to talk or squirm. Pay attention to your own breathing or to your partner's breathing.

Slow your breathing down by taking three or four deep breaths and exhaling forcefully. Make sure that all your muscles are relaxed. Concentrate on each leg individually and imagine that it is sinking into the bed. Picture your shoulders sinking into the bed. Pay attention to the overall sensations of warmth and closeness that wash over you and your partner as you lie together.

You may notice as you spoon breathe for a few minutes that both of you will relax and begin breathing in sync with each other.

You can spoon breathe when clothed or in the nude, in the morning, after work, or at night. A lot of couples like to fall asleep this way. Spoon breathing feels especially good when you are ill. I recommend spooning for ten minutes a day, either when you first wake up or when you go to bed.

♀ Exercise ♂
Eye Gazing

Here is a bonding exercise even more intimate than spoon breathing. It can stop time, open your hearts, and release modesty or defensiveness.

The Exercise　Lie together on your bed and face each other. Wrap your arms comfortably around each other and gaze into each other's eyes for several minutes without talking.

I'll bet you two used to do this when you first met. Remember how good it felt? Enjoy the feelings that come up for you now. How have they grown richer with time?

♀ Exercise ♂
Nurturing

Everyone needs a little nurturing in his or her life. Too often we forget that it is okay to care for our loved one and that it is also okay for her or him to care for us. If one of you has had a bad day, have your partner nurture you.

The Exercise   You can nurture just about anywhere: in bed, on the couch, or on the floor leaning against the couch. One person sits with his back against a wall. The other lies down with her head or torso in that person's lap, in whatever way is comfortable. The person who is sitting tenderly wraps his arms around the person who is lying down.

   Share this embrace for ten minutes. Feel each other's warmth. Listen to each other's breathing. Feel your hearts beat.

♀ Exercise ♂
Lying Together

Have you ever wanted to feel as much of your partner as you could at one time? So often we support each other emotionally, but what is it like to support each other in other ways?

The Exercise   Lie on your back on your bed and have your partner slowly lower herself or himself on top of you, from toes to nose (or thereabouts). The person on top should gradually allow his or her full weight to be supported by the person on the bottom. You can move your heads around until you find a comfortable connection. Lie together for several minutes without talking. You can lie together nude or with clothes on.

   Surprisingly, this position is possible and comfortable for most people. It does not seem to make much of a difference if someone is much larger than the other, since your weight spreads out over a larger area (and the bed). If one of you is much larger than the other, move around until you find a position that works for you. Many people like having their faces very close; others enjoy hearing and feeling their partner's heart beat on their cheek.

♀ Exercise ♂
Palm Energy

This is a wonderful way to become aware of the intangible energy of your relationship.

Sit cross-legged, facing each other. Gaze lovingly into each other's eyes and do not waver. Just as your arms can embrace each other's body's, can your gaze caress each other's souls?

The Exercise Raise your hands and place your palms up against each other. Hold them there for ten seconds. Feel the heat running between you. Now, slowly move your hands apart so that they no longer touch but are just close enough so that you can feel a current of energy flow between you. Concentrate on that flow for five minutes.

♀ Exercise ♂
Palm Energy and Breath Sharing

This exercise may sound innocuous, but it will really knock your socks off! The combination of palm energy and breath sharing sets up an energy exchange that gets your endorphins flowing and takes you to an altered state of consciousness.

The Exercise Begin the palm energy exercise as described above. When you feel the energy flowing between you, lean together as if you were going to kiss. Keep your faces close enough together so that you feel your partner's breath. When one of you breathes in, the other should breathe out. Visualize that breath flowing in a circle: from your mouth to your lungs to your stomach to your pelvis and flowing back into your partner and up through his or her pelvis, stomach, chest, throat and mouth. Now try to reverse this energy circle.

Imagine that you are healing your partner by giving him or her the breath of life.

♀ Exercise ♂
Face Caress

In Chapter 2, you learned to touch yourself in a sensate focus way. You discovered how to touch slowly, sensuously, and without distraction. There are more things to learn when you bring another person into the mix.

When you do any sensate focus caress, one of you should be active and one should be passive. Then switch roles. Alternating activity like this will help you concentrate and will remove the pressure of feeling that you have to "perform." It will help you take greater pleasure in your touch.

These active and passive roles also encourage an important aspect of wholeness, balance, and equality in your relationship. As a relationship progresses, each partner typically takes on roles. They may be task-oriented or emotionally-oriented roles, and often are unconscious. For example, do you cook while your partner does dishes, or are you dependent while your partner is the problem-solver, or is your partner the one who initiates sex? Healing sensate focus exercises give you the opportunity to get outside your usual roles: you are both active and passive, and equally so. As you learn to step outside your usual role, it can be scary. Try not to limit yourself by saying, "I can't possibly be passive during an exercise," or "I'm just not comfortable being active." Branch out and explore a new role. Find new strengths and pleasures. Honor the importance, and responsibility, of equality in a healthy relationship.

When you are active, touch your partner to make it feel good for *you*. This may sound selfish but it is not. This way of touching promotes mutuality: if you both touch for your own pleasure, you will both focus on the same thing (the touch) at the same time. You will be truly, immediately, sharing the experience.

When you are active, in addition to focusing on sensations try to incorporate a mindset of positive, healing energy directed toward your partner, as I mentioned in the introduction. When you are passive, just relax and enjoy the caress. You don't have to respond in any way unless your partner is doing something that bothers you; in that case, speak up gently and clearly. The active and passive roles in the sensate focus exercises foster an intense emotional bond because you begin direct, nonverbal communication instead of talking.

The first sensate focus partner exercise to learn is the face caress. It is a loving and tender exercise.

Before You Begin   To do this caress, you will need a skin lotion that both you and your partner like. You will also need to find a quiet, comfortable room in which to do the exercise. Take the phone off the hook and send the kids to the baby sitter—you need a room in which you will not be disturbed for up to an hour. Have a clock or watch in the room so you can time the exercise.

The Exercise   This exercise is done fully clothed, but you might want to take off your shoes or belt so you are more comfortable. The person who will be active first sits with her back against a headboard or wall, with a pillow on her lap (let's assume the woman is the active partner first). The man should lie between the woman's legs, head on the pillow, face-up. It is important to have the passive partner's face within easy reach of the active partner.

In the face caress you stroke everything from the top of the head to the base of the neck. The active person begins by taking a small amount of the lotion and warming it up in her hand. Then she caresses her partner's face. Remember, a caress is a very slow, light, and sensuous touch. Feel the skin, rather than trying to feel muscles underneath the skin.

Slowly move one or both hands across your partner's forehead and down his cheeks. Caress his chin and on down to the neck. Don't neglect his ears—many people find touching or stroking another person's ears to be a very sensual experience. Caress the bridge of his nose, his eyelids, and the delicate area underneath his eyes.

Caress you partner for around fifteen minutes, then switch roles.

♀ Exercise ♂
Couple Rituals

Another thing you can do to bond better right from the beginning of the relationship is to start your own couple rituals. These are things that you make a commitment to do with each other every day, week, or month. By having rituals together you honor the importance of your relationship. Your purpose and intention, your mindset, is key. With rituals, you can make the familiar unfamiliar and the mundane special. Here are examples of rituals that have been shared by couples I have known.

- If you are religious, attend a worship service together on a regular basis.

- Spend an evening savoring a meal in a particular, favorite restaurant on a regular basis. Or make a special meal together at home on a regular basis.

- If you have a garden, plant a special area together and tend it together.

- Spend an evening every so often reading favorite books or poems aloud. Alternate who reads and who listens each evening.

- Make trips to a "lover's point" to watch the sunset together.

- Take ballroom dancing lessons, then go out dancing on a regular basis.

- Bathe each other and exchange massages.

The key to couple rituals is not *what* you agree to do together, it is that you commit to doing it regularly, that you both participate mutually, and that you both look forward to it. Your ritual could even be an agreement to talk about a particular subject at a particular time: the kids, your life goals, your financial situation, things you think would improve your relationship. These are all rituals that many couples have been successful with. Lovemaking starts before you get to the bedroom, and continues long after you leave it. If you think of everything you do together as adding dimensions to your emotional bond, you will discover new depths for both yourself and your relationship.

♀ Exercise ♂
A New Way of Talking

I hardly ever hear people say positive things about their partners anymore, and it is an absolute shame. Perhaps we have all gotten out of the habit; perhaps we tend to value the negative in conversations; or, perhaps we don't realize the power of positive thought.

For this exercise, first become aware whether you tend to talk with, at, to, or about your partner. When you are talking with your partner, make sure you are talking *with* him or her and not *to* or *at* your partner.

Second, resolve to say something good about your partner to another person. This good thing can be as simple as, "My wife is really great. She makes me laugh all the time" or "You won't believe what my husband did last night. It made me so happy."

As part of this exercise, try to do something nice for your partner that is sure to inspire this type of thought and comment on his or her part.

Feedback After the Exercises

An important activity that fosters intimacy as a couple is talking about each of the exercises in this book after you do it. As you work through the exercises in this and in the next chapters, take a few minutes after each exercise and talk about it. As you talk, respect each other by listening intently and not interrupting. Ask each other questions along these lines: How did you feel during the exercise? Which part of the exercise was most enjoyable for you? What percent of the time were you able to concentrate during the touching? Is there anything about the exercise you didn't like? Would you like to do this exercise again? What changes would you like to make?

Mutuality, Intimacy, and Commitment

I cannot say it enough: the keys to sexual healing are mutuality, intimacy, and commitment. The sexual healing exercises teach you these three things. You learn to promote mutuality (movement toward common goals) because in the exercises you both pay attention to the same thing at the same time. The physical closeness you experience during the exercises leads to emotional closeness, which deepens your intimacy. And there are two ways in which the exercises contribute to commitment.

The first is that a big part of making a commitment to each other is committing to change. We get older, we grow wiser, and we evolve from our experiences—we are dynamic processes, and our relationships must change as we do. You have begun the exercises in this book because you both want something in your relationship to change. That is a commitment.

The second way in which the exercises help to develop commitment is that when you agree to do an exercise together at a certain time, and you actually follow through and do the exercise that you have agreed on, you are learning commitment in small, painless steps.

The exercises in this chapter and in this book are not the only things that can bring you together as a couple. Meaningful life events, such as the birth of a baby, can be touchstone moments of your love for each other. Unfortunately, tragic events such as the loss of a loved one can bring you together, too. Do you have to go through adversity or tragedy to reach intimacy and healing? Of course not. If you build a strong bond from the beginning, your union is more likely to withstand the tragedies and disasters that happen to all of us at some time in our lives. If you build an intimate bond now, it will grow to be strong enough to sustain and heal you if tragedy should strike.

What's Love Got to Do with It?

You have probably noticed that I don't talk too much about love. I may have even written this whole chapter without mentioning it! Isn't it the most important factor in whether or not a couple stays together?

Surprisingly, no. We equate sex and love in this culture, but many cultures don't. Even in this culture, the idea that you should be "in love" with someone before you get married and have sex is a fairly recent development. My reason for not emphasizing love is that most often it is vague, it means different things to different people, and it is often mislabeled. Sure, it is great if you have feelings of love for your partner, even better if you are hopelessly "in love." But character, values, respect, and even general affection and liking are more important for the success of the relationship. The excuse, "I no longer feel in love with you," as a reason for breaking up may not be enough of a reason for you to end a romantic partnership. Instead, if you share mutual trust and respect, consider trying to salvage the relationship by using the exercises in this book. Wouldn't it be an interesting world if values and respect instead of appearance and money were sexual turn-ons and the requirements for romantic love?

Chapter 4

Sexual Fitness

**Y**ou don't have to be an athlete to make great love —that's what is so wonderful about lovemaking. Anybody, at any level of fitness, can have satisfying sexual intimacy. If you have physical problems or limitations, you can still make love by adjusting your position, limiting the amount of time you spend, or eliminating certain activities that cause you physical problems. All it takes is some creativity and listening to your body.

There are a few simple things you can do to get in better "love-making shape." I call them "sexual fitness exercises" but don't worry; they don't work up a sweat. By strengthening the muscles in your genitals and pelvic area and learning how to relax the rest of your body, you can spend more delicious time in intimate, aroused lovemaking.

General Fitness

Before we get into specific pelvic exercises, let's talk for a minute about general aerobic fitness. Are you in great physical condition— a triathlete or marathon runner? Are you a fitness disaster area—a true couch potato? Most of us are somewhere in between. To receive the most healing from this program, you need to have a basic level of general fitness. What does this mean?

If you smoke, please do your best to stop now or begin tapering off. It is a proven fact that cigarette smoking is one of the worst things you can do for your love life. Nicotine is a stimulant that restricts blood flow to the small blood vessels in your skin. It erodes your ability to feel sensations and impairs circulation to the point that many smokers have difficulty having orgasms and, for male smokers, getting erections.

If you don't exercise on a regular basis, start walking. Try to take a brisk walk for fifteen or twenty minutes every day. Any exercise you can get will energize you and prepare you for lovemaking. As always, consult your physician before you begin any exercise program.

Nutrition

I do believe that eating and drinking, like making love, are two of the greatest pleasures in life. Simple pleasures like these are largely the things in life that you share with your partner. I also believe you can enjoy great foods and drink great wine without becoming obese or an alcoholic. Have you heard of the so-called French paradox? The French are renowned for eating fatty foods and drinking wine, and yet they are healthier and in better shape than Americans. There are a lot of possible explanations for this, one being that the French tend not to snack between meals and, while growing up, they exercise more. And don't forget, the French are famous for their abilities as lovers as well. Could it be that they know something we don't about how pleasurable eating, drinking, and lovemaking fit into a healthy, cohesive lifestyle?

On a more serious note, there is no doubt that nutrition is critical to maintaining a healthy body and overall well-being, so it is important to make sure your nutritional needs are being met.

Are you severely overweight? I don't mean "pleasingly plump," which is normal and *not* unhealthy. If you are clinically overweight, 20 to 40 percent or more above the ideal weight for your height, it may put a damper on a satisfying sex life. That much excess weight can directly impair your ability not only to move around during lovemaking, but to feel sensations in the genital area and to have orgasms and erections. Men who are severely overweight often find that the fat layer over their pelvic area reduces their penis length by several inches, which becomes a direct cause of problems in making love.

If you need to lose weight, don't beat yourself up over it. Focus on appreciating your body and caring for it, not abusing yourself about it. Start eating healthy fruits and vegetables, watch your fat intake, and begin walking every day. If you need a more stringent diet or exercise program, please see your physician for advice. It could be the single best thing you do for yourself.

Drugs

Many people believe that certain drugs are aphrodisiacs—drugs that stimulate sexual desire. But aphrodisiacs do not exist. Sharing an occasional glass or two of wine or champagne with your partner may help the two of you loosen up and let go of the week's stresses, but I would not recommend this as a regular practice. I have seen alcohol do irreparable harm to lovemaking and loving relationships. Alcohol use causes severe problems with erections, ejaculation, desire, and orgasm.

Some people report that they feel more sexual desire if they smoke marijuana or snort cocaine. Any positive sexual effects from these drugs are short-term. The long-term effect of all illegal drugs is to impair your ability to make love, on top of ruining your physical and mental health.

What about prescription drugs? Impaired sexual response is a side effect of many prescription drugs, including ulcer medications, high-blood pressure medications, and even antihistamines. If you are concerned about a current prescription you may be taking, consult your physician to discuss your options.

I am not a health nut or fitness buff, and generally prefer to spend my time talking about the positive aspects of lovemaking;

still this is advice I must give: if you want your lovemaking to be better so that you share a powerful, healing bond with your partner, stop smoking, moderate your eating, drinking, and prescription medications, get *some* exercise, and don't use illegal drugs.

Sex Muscle Exercises

The first stage of sexual fitness is getting yourself in reasonable physical shape. The second stage of sexual fitness is getting your "sex muscles" in good shape. The PC or pubococcygeus muscle group runs from the pelvic bone in the front of your body to your tailbone in the rear. This muscle group supports the floor of your pelvic cavity and your pelvic organs, and more intriguingly, is the key to longer-lasting, fulfilling sexual union.

There are special exercises that men and women can do to strengthen, tone, and gain expert control over this muscle group.

♀ Exercise ♂
PC Muscle for Women

Before You Begin Before you can begin to exercise your PC muscle, you must locate it. Place one of your fingers lightly against your vaginal lips or inside your vagina up to the first knuckle. Pretend you are urinating and you want to stop the flow. The muscle that tightens around your finger when you do this is the PC muscle group. Internally, you should feel a drawing together or a drawing upward in your vaginal and pelvic area.

When you squeeze the muscle, make sure you are not also tensing your abdomen or thigh muscles at the same time. Also, remember to keep breathing as you squeeze and relax. You should be able to tighten your PC muscle without it being visible to anyone looking at you.

The Exercise   Once you have located the muscle, there's no need to keep your hand on it as you tighten and relax. So, three times a day, spend a few minutes flexing and relaxing your PC muscle twenty times. Breathe deeply and steadily throughout. You can do these flexes anytime, anywhere—driving your car, waiting in line, brushing your teeth.

If you are older, overweight, or have had children, you may want to start with as few as five or ten repetitions, then work your way up to twenty. The PC muscle tires easily and may not relax fully each time you flex when you first start, but it will tone up quickly.

A strong PC muscle has many benefits for women. It tightens and tones the vagina, and gives you better bladder control. It also helps tone the vagina after giving birth. (These exercises were first developed by an obstetrician, Dr. A. H. Kegel, to control incontinence in pregnant women and women who had just given birth. They are often referred to as Kegel exercises.) A strong PC muscle also makes it easier to have orgasms. In both women and men, flexing the PC muscle at the moment of orgasm intensifies the orgasm. This is because when your PC muscle is in shape, more blood can flow to the genital area and more blood can be expelled from the genital area during orgasm. And aside from all of the reasons given above, doing this exercise is fun and feels good.

♀ Exercise ♂
PC Muscle for Men

Before You Begin   To locate your PC muscle, lightly place two fingers behind your testicles. Now imagine that you are urinating and want to stop the flow. The muscle that you squeeze internally to stop the flow is the PC muscle. Practice stopping and starting your urination a couple of times so that you know where this muscle group is located.

The Exercise   Every day, three times a day, flex and relax this muscle group twenty times. Now that you know where the muscle is, you won't have to touch it to exercise it. Make sure that you have isolated the muscle and are not tightening your abdomen, buttocks, or your facial muscles during this exercise. Keep every other muscle in your body as relaxed as you can, and remember to breathe evenly as you squeeze and relax. It is easy to do this muscle exercise. Tightening and relaxing this muscle should feel good; you may even feel slightly aroused because when you exercise this muscle you are increasing blood flow into the genital area.

It may take you a while to work up to twenty repetitions; if you are older or overweight, you may want to start with only five or ten repetitions, then work your way up. Don't do more than twenty repetitions at a time, or your PC muscle may get sore. It will take about three weeks for your PC muscle to get in shape, and then you really need to do this exercise for the rest of your life. It is an important part of maintaining your sexual fitness. Men whose PC muscle is in good shape can have more enjoyable erections, more sensation in the genital area, better ejaculation control, stronger orgasms, and even multiple orgasms.

Another important benefit of the PC muscle exercise for men is improved prostate health. The stronger your PC muscle is, the stronger your ejaculation will be, which means that your prostate gland is more likely to expel all of its contents during ejaculation. Men who have consistent, complete ejaculations tend to have fewer problems with prostate enlargement.

If you are using the sexual healing program in this book to solve a specific sexual problem, the PC muscle exercises are essential for you. In therapy, the clients who learned most quickly to have orgasms, control their ejaculations, and have erections were those who were consistent about exercising the PC muscle. Have I sold you on this? I hope so.

♀ Exercise ♂
Advanced PC Muscle
for Men and Women

After you have done the basic PC muscle exercise for three weeks, try this advanced exercise. In addition to twenty quick repetitions, add ten slow repetitions. You should be able to feel your PC muscle slowly suck in and then slowly push back out. Try to gradually tense the muscle for five seconds, hold it for five seconds, and then push back out for five seconds. The first time, you may only be able to do this once or twice. Eventually you can work up to ten repetitions. It may take you days or weeks—the time doesn't matter, the improved muscle tone does.

♀ Exercise ♂
Pelvic Thrusts

The third stage of sexual fitness is to have strength and control of the voluntary muscles in your pelvic area. People who are experiencing sexual problems often unconsciously tighten the muscles in their pelvic area. The next three exercises—pelvic thrusts, rolls, and tilts—are for your abdomen, buttocks, and thigh muscles. They will help loosen you up and release the tension from those areas. They are good for both men and women.

Pelvic thrusts can be done either lying down or standing. The idea is to rock your pelvis from back to front without moving any other parts of your body. It is especially important to keep from tensing your stomach or leg muscles.

The Exercise   If you are lying down, put your knees up and rock your buttocks slowly up and down so they are the only part of you that moves off the floor. Do it as quickly or slowly as you like and as many times as you like. You can rock to music if you wish, or vary the speed of your rocking.

The important thing is to keep all your other muscles relaxed and to keep your breathing regular. Do not hold your breath. To make sure you are breathing correctly, it may be helpful to grunt or make some noise with each lift. If you want to do pelvic thrusts while standing or walking, simply stand and rock your pelvis back and forth, or, as you walk, consciously thrust your pelvis forward with each step.

♀ Exercise ♂
Pelvic Rolls

Pelvic rolls are similar to thrusts. Either lying down or standing, roll your hips backward-sideways-forward-sideways in a continuous motion. Think of Elvis Presley. If you have difficulty getting the hang of this movement, buy a hula hoop and practice with that. Practice rolls at different speeds. Practice rolling as slowly as you possibly can. And remember to keep the muscles in your buttocks, legs, and abdomen relaxed.

Combine thrusts and rolls and do them to music if it feels good. Try to do a series of these thrusts and rolls for about ten minutes every day. Close your eyes so that you can really feel your body. The secret to doing these exercises is to roll and thrust your pelvis while still staying loose. Men, especially, tend to have tight hip muscles. Loosening them up can often increase your ability to become sexually aroused and have erections.

♀ Exercise ♂
Pelvic Tilts

The third pelvic exercise is the pelvic tilt. Lie on your back with your knees up. Keep your lower back on the floor, and practice tilting your pelvis up and down. This is similar to the pelvic thrust but your lower back stays on the floor and you have a smaller range of movement. Pelvic tilts can also be done standing up.

Simply keep your lower back in the same position and tilt your pelvis back and forth.

———————

Worried about back problems? In my experience, most people can do pelvic thrusts, rolls, and tilts without risk, especially if they do them slowly. If you have back problems, especially in your lower back, go easy and consult your physician before attempting them.

A number of other physical exercises can be beneficial to love-making, particularly those that involve stretching, squatting, and spreading your legs. In general, any sport or physical exercise bene-fits your love life because it improves your cardiovascular condition-ing, flexibility, body image, and general physical health and well-being. So if you already have a fitness program you are com-fortable with, incorporate the PC muscle exercises and the pelvic exercises into this program, and continue having fun.

Photograph by
Michael Geringer

Chapter 5

Becoming a Sexual Healer
—Beginning Exercises

I n this chapter, you will learn sensual and sexual exercises to do with a partner. By now you have discovered how to touch yourself pleasurably and how to create and foster the intimate bond with your partner. Now it is time to learn from the healing that surrogate partners practice with their clients.

The therapy that surrogate partners practice is powerful and unique, but there are many misconceptions about what surrogate partners do. Many people consider sexual surrogates essentially prostitutes, sex workers who are paid to have sex with people they don't know. In fact, nothing could be further from the truth.

What Happens in Sex Therapy?

When a married couple comes in for sex therapy, the focus is on keeping the couple together. No reputable sex therapist or marriage counselor would try to split up a couple, except in cases of abuse. Certainly, no therapist would advise one member of that couple to have sex with a third person! Instead, sex therapists ask couples to do certain touching and bonding exercises together in the privacy of their own home or other private place, such as a hotel room. The exercises range from simple and sensual to more sexual, and many of the exercises in this book are based on sex therapy exercises.

How Surrogate Partners Heal

When a single person comes to a sex therapist for problems such as lack of desire, or orgasm, arousal, or erection difficulties, this single person is in a bind. He or she needs to do the same exercises the couple would do, but has no partner to practice them with. To address single people's needs, many sex therapists work with trained, professional surrogate partners who act as the client's partner during therapy. Professional surrogates always work under the supervision of a licensed therapist.

For twelve years, from 1980 to 1992, I worked as a professional surrogate partner and personally treated hundreds of clients, mostly men with erection problems or premature ejaculation. It was during that time that my colleagues and I developed many of the exercises you will learn in this book.

I was inspired to become a surrogate partner so that I could help heal others. It is a helping profession, akin to teaching and nursing. In fact, it has much more in common with professions like nursing and counseling than it does with prostitution or other sex-industry occupations, which poorly informed people often compare it to. I also became a surrogate partner because I believed that sex therapy worked, that it changed lives. I believe that lovemaking in certain relationships can be a life-affirming and possibly life-changing experience.

Based on my years of surrogate experience, I strongly believe the relationship between client and surrogate is a healing one. It is not the best of all healing scenarios, since neither person is the other's physical choice and emotional mate, and the relationship is artificial and time-limited. Nevertheless, a great deal of emotional, physical, sexual, and spiritual healing has taken place in client-surrogate relationships. I've even known people whose lives have been changed dramatically by one episode of lovemaking. You will read about some of these cases later, especially in the chapter on chronic illness.

So what do surrogates and clients actually do? In the first session, I would begin by sitting and talking with the client, similar to a first therapy session or a first date. Then, usually during the first session, we would take turns doing the exercise called the face caress that you learned in Chapter 3. The client and I would meet with the therapist before and after our session, which usually lasted about an hour. By the second session, most clients were comfortable with nudity, so we would take off our clothes and do a sensate focus back caress. If the client was comfortable, the next session would be a front caress, and then a genital caress. Depending on the client's problem, we would then progress to the more advanced sexual exercises you will read about later in this book.

As a surrogate partner, it was my job to create a relaxing atmosphere for my clients. Keep in mind that they were very nervous. I taught a lot of them how to breathe, relax their muscles, and do PC muscle exercises. Meanwhile, I had to be alert to any signs of their anxiety. If a client became too anxious, we would stop the exercise and back up to something comfortable. I also had to figure out whether the client was responding normally or had some kind of physical problem. There were multiple things going on that I had to be aware of. In addition, I had to be ready, willing, and able to do an exercise when I came to work—but I also had to be myself and not fake a response.

Since surrogate partner work is a healing profession, you are very subject to burnout. My work as a surrogate partner meant a lot to me, but it is the type of job you cannot do forever. I eventually reached a point where I couldn't do it anymore. Most people think I stopped working as a surrogate because I got tired of impersonal sex. Actually the opposite is true—it is too personal. You run the danger of caring too much about your clients and you take their problems home with you.

What You Can Learn from Surrogate Partners

As a beginning sexual healer, what can you learn from my experience? Some of the things you can learn are very concrete, and some are intangible. Here are some of the concrete things you can learn. The first seems pretty basic but it eludes a lot of people. That is, if you want to be a sexual healer for yourself and your partner, you must schedule a time to do exercises together and both agree on that time. Second, if you agree to the scheduled time you should be ready to fully engage in it—mentally, physically, and emotionally. If you or your partner are not emotionally or physically prepared to do so, recognize this and don't pursue the exercise; and if you have already begun, stop and backtrack. Third, to be a sexual healer you should have a comfortable room that is completely free of distractions.

Now, the intangibles, starting with attitude. Remember the motivational talk I gave you in the introduction, about the healing mindset? You can sexually heal yourself and your partner if you stay in that mindset. As a surrogate I always did my best to convey the nonverbal expectation that the client would be fine and everything would be all right. Remember that another big part of that attitude is what you *don't* convey: you don't convey anxiety or performance pressure about erections, arousal, or desire. The best way to describe my professional sexual healing is to say that for the space of one hour my client and I were absolutely absorbed and involved with each other. As lovers, you and your partner will experience the added force of working to be sexual healers for each other, with each other.

In Chapter 2 you learned how to touch in a sensate focus way. Then I showed you the basics of partner touching in Chapter 3, including the active and passive roles and how to interact in a pressure-free way. With those basics under your belt, so to speak, you two are ready to move on to more intimate and pleasing caresses: the back caress, the front caress, and the genital caress. Let them awaken your sexual healing capacity!

♀ Exercise ♂
Back Caress

The back caress introduces several new elements. It is the first sensate focus exercise that involves parts of the body that you may already associate with sexual arousal, for example, the buttocks. It is also the first sensate focus exercise that you do in the nude.

When my clients and I did the back caress, it was the first time we had seen each other nude, so it was exciting. For you and your partner, nudity may be old hat and you may be completely comfortable with each other. On the other hand, seeing each other nude may not be a comfortable part of your relationship, and if it is not, please compromise so that you are both comfortable. For example, dim the lights or drape a sheet over you.

Before You Begin Prepare your bed, or some other comfortable place with plenty of room for both of you to stretch out. As always, make sure you have a quiet room where you won't be disturbed. You may also like to use a large towel and some talcum powder.

The Exercise The back caress includes the entire back of the body from the neck to the feet, but not the genitals. Spend about five minutes spoon breathing to relax together. Then, decide which partner will be active first (let's say it is the man).

The passive partner lies face down, on top of the towel, in a comfortable position. She may keep her arms at her sides or underneath her head. The active partner lies next to her, maintaining as much body contact as possible during the exercise. Both of you should remember the basic sensate focus instructions—focus, breathe, relax.

The active person begins by stroking his partner's back with one hand. Start at the neck. Slowly run your palm or fingers over the shoulder blades and then down the spine. Don't forget: touch to make it feel good for you. Explore the sensuality of your partner's back with different strokes, using all parts of your hand—your fingertips, palm, knuckles. Remember, this is not a massage; use your hand to feel as good as you possibly can by touching your partner's body. Focus on sending a sense of healing goodwill toward your partner without speaking any words.

When you are the active partner, caress your partner's back, buttocks, and legs for your own pleasure. Think of your partner's body as a playground and touch anything that feels good to you. You will maximize your ability to focus on sensations if you close your eyes during the caress.

The way that I usually do the back caress is to snuggle up against my partner and use my hand to reach as many parts of his back as I can. Then I change positions so that I can caress his legs and feet. I usually use some type of baby powder for this caress. It increases the pleasing sensations for me since my hands tend to perspire, which makes my touch a little rough. Try for yourself whether powder or lotion enhance your sensations.

Remember to stroke your partner slowly. If you have trouble focusing, consciously slow your caressing motion down to half the speed it was before. If thoughts about what your partner is feeling intrude, bring your mind back to the exact point of contact between your skin and your partner's skin.

Pay attention to how the different body parts feel when you slowly stroke them with your palm versus your fingertips. Some areas on the back of the body that feel especially good to touch include the back of the neck, the spine, and the tender skin of the thighs underneath the buttocks. Pay attention to temperature, texture, contour, contrast, and shape. Run your fingers around the depression at the base of your partner's spine. Slide the tip of one finger slowly up your partner's backbone. You may want to conclude the caress with a final loving or sensual gesture, like a soft pinch on the earlobe or running your fingers through your partner's hair.

As a variation you can use your upper body to caress, in addition to your fingers and hand. Use your hair, face, or chest to caress if you can do it for your own pleasure and not worry about whether your partner enjoys it.

If you feel or see your partner's body tensing during this caress (for example, as you touch her thighs, you see the muscles tighten, or she moves around) lightly pinch or press down on the thigh as a signal to your partner to relax. Remind her to breathe, and continue gently with the caress.

When you are the passive partner, enjoy yourself. Soak up the sensations like a sponge. Breathe evenly and relax your muscles. Keep your mind on the exact point of contact where your partner strokes you. Try not to move; just passively accept stimulation into your body. The only time you need to verbally communicate with your partner is if he or she does something that bothers you.

Spend about twenty minutes each in the active role. Do some spoon breathing between role changes and then again at the end of the exercise.

———

Some books recommend that the active person straddle his partner's back and use both hands to do this caress. I find there is much more feeling when the caress is done lying next to your partner, with lots of contact and with a minimum of effort. In this position you feel very connected to each other and can focus on healing without being distracted by a pain or muscle cramp. Doing a back caress in a traditional massage position (straddling the partner) also tends to set up the exercise as a performance situation right from the start; this conveys the expectation to my partner that he must respond.

Sometimes people think it is selfish to either touch for your own pleasure or to passively accept caressing without responding. The active and passive roles don't restrict you. If you are truly focusing and enjoying yourself, the roles free you to allow you to totally experience the touch without pressure. Remember that when you and your partner both focus on the same thing at the same time, you create that state of mutuality that deepens your relationship.

It may be easier to feel that you are healing your partner when you take the active role. You should also be aware that your passive or receptive attitude is healing also. You are giving your partner the gift of allowing him or her to heal you.

If you become sexually aroused during the back caress, fine. Just enjoy the arousal and bring your mind back to the exact point of contact. Try not to be concerned with sexual arousal yet. Right now you are cultivating a healing touch so that it becomes second nature whenever you touch your partner. You are laying a foundation so that when you move on to exercises that are more sexual, you will exude this healing touch even when you are extremely aroused.

♀ Exercise ♂
Front Caress

The front caress lavishes attention on the whole front of the body, from the head to toe. It includes the genitals, but only in a casual way, which means that you don't spend any more time caressing the genitals than you do any other area. The front caress does not include penetrating the vagina, only stroking outside it. This is a sensual exercise, not a sexual one, and it is not intended to arouse your partner. The instructions are the same as for the back caress: one of you caresses the other for twenty minutes, then you switch.

Before You Begin   Make sure you are in a warm, quiet room free from distractions. You will need a towel, talcum powder, baby oil or another sensuous lubricant. Some people use massage oil, KY Jelly, mineral oil, or baby oil. I tend to use oil-based products because oil warms up more rapidly on the body and lasts longer.

The Exercise   Get centered together with a few minutes of spoon breathing. Then the passive partner lies on his or her back in a relaxed position (let's say it is the man, this time). The active person lies next to him, maintaining as much full-body contact as possible. When you are active, try resting your hand or your cheek on your partner's chest and listening to his heartbeat for a few minutes. Before you caress, sprinkle talcum powder on your partner's body and on your hand if you tend to perspire.

The active person begins slowly stroking the passive person's body, beginning with his face, neck, shoulders, and arms. She moves down across his chest, stroking stomach, abdomen, and genitals, then caresses his thighs, calves, and even his feet.

When you are active, caress as slowly and delicately as possible. Caress in a flowing manner—don't jump from the feet to the head but proceed down the body, stroking one area at a time. It is also important to maintain loving contact with your partner's body. You can help your partner relax by keeping your hand on him as much as possible and avoiding surprising or startling touches.

Throughout the caress, touch for your own pleasure. Use your palm, fingers, or the back of your hand or arm. Toward the end of the caress you may want to kneel and caress your partner's body with your face, hair, or chest. This can be very sensuous and pleasurable. Don't concern yourself with what your partner is thinking or feeling during the caress. He will tell you if something makes him uncomfortable. Simply focus on bringing out that healing energy toward your partner. If you caress too rapidly or roughly, your partner will feel pressured to respond. If you caress for your own enjoyment, focusing as much as you can, your partner will enjoy the caress too, and healing energy will pass between you.

When you are passive, your only task is to relax and enjoy the caress. The only time you need to say anything is if something bothers you. If you feel yourself tensing, slow your breathing and let your body sink into the bed. Focus on the exact point of contact, receiving your partner's touch and receiving the *energy* in her touch. See if you can close your eyes and focus so intently on your partner's touch that you can no longer tell where his or her hand ends and your body begins. Can you feel heat radiating through your body from your partner's hand?

To finish the front caress, whoever is active lies on top of or right beside the passive person and listens to his or her heart. Spend about twenty minutes apiece on the front caress, and spoon breathe in between role changes and at the end of the exercise.

♀ Exercise ♂
Genital Caress

Before You Begin   Come together in a quiet room, with a towel and a sensuous lubricant you both like.

The Exercise   Center yourselves with spoon breathing. Then have each partner choose a focusing caress, either a short back caress or a short front caress, to help you relax before the main exercise. The passive partner lies comfortably on his or her back, with legs slightly spread. His or her arms can be at the sides or under the head.

The active partner begins by caressing the front of the passive partner's body with powder, as in the front caress. This time, however, you spend at least half the time caressing your partner's genitals. After about ten minutes of the front caress, wipe the powder off your hand and warm up some lubricant in your palm. Slowly begin to caress your partner's genitals with your fingers.

If your partner is a woman, use lots of lubrication and slowly stroke your fingers over her outer vaginal lips, inner vaginal lips, perineum, and clitoris. Channel your attention into each stroke. Carefully insert your finger inside her vagina. Feel the warmth and texture of her vaginal walls and the muscles surrounding the vaginal opening. If your mind drifts, bring it back to your touch. Caress for ten to fifteen minutes.

As part of this caress, lie between your partner's legs as you caress her and learn what her genitals look like as well as feel like. Take this opportunity to learn every hair, every fold of skin. If you feel yourself becoming mechanical or bored with the caress, slow down your strokes.

If your passive partner is a man, caress the front of his body for about ten minutes and then warm some lubricant in your hand. Slowly caress his penis and scrotum with your fingers. Don't try to turn him on—caress so it feels as good as possible for you. Slowly move your fingers around the shaft and head of the penis. Run your fingers around each testicle. Focus on what you are feeling; if your mind drifts off to something else, bring it back to your touch.

It doesn't matter whether your partner has an erection during the genital caress. A soft penis feels just as good as an erect one— the sensations are not better or worse, just different. Experience exactly what the skin feels like on the different areas of your partner's genitals. If he becomes aroused and ejaculates, wipe him off and continue the caress. Caress for ten to fifteen minutes.

When you are the passive partner, close your eyes. As you receive the genital caress, focus, breathe, and relax. Allow yourself to soak up all the sensations like a sponge. The only time you need to say anything is if your partner does something that hurts or bothers you.

In between role changes, and again at the end of the exercise, come together in full-body spoon breathing. After the caress, be sure to talk with each other about how each of you felt during the exercise.

Now that you have tapped into basic sexual healing with caresses of the back, the front, and the genitals, you are ready to explore the more sexual and advanced healing exercises in Chapters 7 and 8. As you develop your sexual healing repertoire, keep in mind that you can always come back to these exercises. Front and back caresses are wonderful ways to cherish and honor each other's bodies.

Chapter 6

Using Lovemaking to Heal Emotional and Mental Problems

**I**n this chapter, you will learn to use lovemaking to heal anxiety and depression, as well as mental problems such as lack of concentration. You will also learn to heal harmful attitudes, such as poor self-image and chronic negativity.

Stopping Stress and Anxiety

The aspects of lovemaking that calm and relax you and those that strengthen your sense of self also help to allay anxiety. In Chapter 3, you learned relaxation and bonding exercises with your partner. Here are exercises you can do by yourself to really increase that ability to relax and activate the benevolent energies of the parasympathetic nervous system. Relaxation training is one of the few areas of psychology that has been proven effective (sex therapy is another). So take advantage of these time-tested exercises. You may also benefit from this heightened relaxation before embarking on the advanced sexual healer exercises with your partner.

♀ Exercise ♂
Belly Breathing

Proper breathing is the basis of life—and of *feeling* alive. The oxygen we take in with every breath is our lifeline, but a lot of us don't breathe properly, and this can create or exacerbate anxiety and sexual problems. The more anxious and pent up we become, the more constricted our breathing and the less oxygen we take in. Before you do anything else, make sure the way you breathe relaxes you. Here is a simple breathing exercise you should do every day. It is called belly breathing.

The Exercise Lie comfortably on a bed, on your back. Loosen any tight clothing. Place one hand on your stomach or abdomen and the other on your heart. Now take a deep, slow breath that you can feel all the way down to your abdomen. Breathe as if you are drawing breath down through your body, into your legs and toes. This type of breath will cause your abdomen to expand and rise; when you exhale, it will contract.

As you breathe, inhaling and exhaling should be one continuous process. Don't hold your breath after you inhale. Feel the air flowing all the way into your lungs and all the way out. Visualize that air as a white light flowing in and out of you, not only relaxing you but energizing you. If you want to, rest after each exhale.

To "belly breathe," take two deep belly breaths and then breathe normally for about a minute. Take two belly breaths again and breathe normally for another minute. Repeat this pattern for about ten minutes.

♀ Exercise ♂
Deep Muscle Relaxation

Sexual healing relies on deeply relaxed muscles. But didn't I say earlier that your muscles should be in good shape to make satisfying love? Of course! Both are true: You need to combine the healthy energy and stamina that comes from fitness with as much freedom from anxiety as possible to make pleasurable, healing love.

Deep muscle relaxation is a well-known antidote for anxiety, with a special benefit in lovemaking. When you have mastered it, you will know your own body so well that if a muscle group becomes too tense during lovemaking, you will immediately notice it. You can then consciously, immediately relax so that muscle tension won't interfere with your lovemaking.

The Exercise   Lie down on your bed, on your back, in a comfortable position. Starting with your right foot, then your left foot, tighten each group of muscles in your body and hold them as tight as you can for a few seconds, then relax them. Remember to breathe as you do this exercise.

Work your way up your entire body, tensing and relaxing each muscle group: feet, calves, thighs, entire legs, buttocks, abdomen, stomach, chest, neck, hands, lower arms, upper arms, entire arms, and face.

Severe Anxiety

Does extreme anxiety when you think about sex prevent you from making love? Psychologists have made great strides in treating these severe types of specific anxieties, which are called phobias. They use a treatment called systematic desensitization. The fearful person is presented with the thing he or she fears (the stimulus) in a very mild form; he or she is then exposed to increasingly stronger forms of the stimulus, while being trained to relax with breathing and muscle control.

In a similar way, this program offers a series of exercises that start out as relaxing and sensual and gradually become more sexual. For example, if you have a great deal of anxiety related to sexuality, do the belly breathing and deep muscle relaxation exercises every day. Then, work through the exercises by yourself in Chapter 2. Next, try the partner bonding exercises in Chapter 3. Then move to the beginning sexual healer exercises in Chapter 5. Soon you will notice that you experience less and less anxiety. There is only one precaution that I would give you: do not proceed with an exercise if your anxiety does not decrease. If you get a few minutes into an exercise and find yourself unable to relax, stop and go back to an earlier exercise that you know you are comfortable with.

The relaxation process I recommend has much in common with that described by Herbert Benson in his classic book *The Relaxation Response* (1975). According to Benson, four things are necessary for the relaxation response to occur: a mental device, quiet, a comfortable position, and a receptive attitude. In these sexual healing exercises, sensate focus provides the device that keeps your mind occupied, the exercises are done in a quiet room and a comfortable position, and when you do exercises with your partner you alternate between taking a passive or receptive and an active or expressive role.

Performance Anxiety

In most areas of life we are taught to work hard and achieve. Those who succeed in school and at jobs are valued by society. They are the go-getters and self-made successes. And from childhood on we are encouraged to compete, an attitude which often helps us achieve work or school goals (though possibly at the expense of our mental health).

Lovemaking, however, is an area in which this performance orientation has only negative effects. For example, men who have been successful in work often encounter difficulties with erections as they age. Success in business often means thinking many steps ahead of what you are doing in the present. In sexuality, thinking ahead stops the connection to sensual experience and leads to feelings of anxiety and pressure to perform, which results in erection failure.

If you have issues with thinking of sex as a performance, several features of these exercises will help you: the fact that you stay in the here and now, the active and passive roles, and the fact that you touch for yourself. These aspects of the exercises should go a long way toward healing destructive performance anxiety impulses. I suggest beginning with these breathing and relaxation exercises, then going to the touching and bonding exercises of the first chapters and, finally, working your way through the sexual healer exercises.

Lifting Depression

Depression is another enemy of satisfying lovemaking. In fact, one of the common symptoms of depression is temporary loss of sex drive. The solution for depression is to take action. The best treatment for depression is to do something physical—and lovemaking is one of the best physical things you can do.

Sexual arousal is a powerful antidote to depression. It works because our bodies affect our minds in a number of positive ways. The study of how changes in the body affect the mind is called somatopsychology or somatopsychics (you can read more about this in Chapter 9). This is the idea that physically moving the body into certain positions or performing certain physical activities influences our psychological states, particularly our moods, and particularly depression. Since many people are not familiar with somatopsychology, let me offer some examples and analogies.

When we move our facial muscles into expressions of emotions, to some degree we experience those emotions. Studies in psychology laboratories have shown that people who are instructed to turn up the corners of their mouths and hold them that way and are not told why report more feelings of happiness than people who are not asked to change their expressions (and you wondered what went on in those labs!). Another example is one way many women have learned to have orgasms: by imitating the facial expressions and body position changes of orgasm, they eventually bring on orgasms. Last, studies consistently show that physical exercise, such as jogging, aerobics, or bicycling, decreases depression and anxiety and increases positive emotional states.

The field of bioenergetic psychotherapy also supports the idea that the body influences the mind. Bioenergetics, as described by Alexander Lowen (who founded the field based on the theories of Wilhelm Reich), is a type of therapy that uses the idea that psychological conflicts are expressed in the ways in which we hold our bodies. By helping clients change their body positions, bioenergetic therapists hope to help them understand and resolve those conflicts.

On a simple, biochemical level, physical exercise stimulates the production of endorphins, brain chemicals that kill pain and promote euphoria. During states of sexual arousal, we also produce these natural euphorics.

So if you suffer from mild to moderate depression and would like to use lovemaking to help, the first step is, don't wait until you feel sexual to make love—you could be waiting a long time. Start scheduling time for yourself and your partner to do the exercises in this book. Forget spontaneity; until you jumpstart your sex drive you will have to schedule time for lovemaking. Believe it or not, one of the best ways of coping with depression is routine, something you can plan for at the same time every day—and what better thing to count on than a comforting touching exercise, either for you and your partner or you alone.

I recommend starting with the self-touch exercises in Chapter 2. Then do the bonding exercises in Chapter 3 and the sexual fitness exercises in Chapter 4. After you've done those, try the following three exercises by yourself to see if you can spark a little sexual energy and charge up that libido. When you do any exercise, just pay attention to how you feel. Don't pressure yourself to become aroused or reach orgasm.

♀ Exercise ♂
Arousal Awareness

To develop arousal awareness, think of your sexual arousal on a scale from one to ten, with one being not aroused at all, and ten being orgasm. Levels two or three are mild twinges of arousal, but arousal is not really constant. Levels four and five are a constant low level of arousal, and levels six and seven are steady, moderate arousal. At six or seven you should be starting to feel that you'd like this exercise to continue. At level eight, if you had to talk, you would sound somewhat out of breath. Level nine is feeling very close to orgasm. Anything beyond level nine is feeling that orgasm is inevitable.

For men, it is important that you notice how aroused you feel, regardless of how strong your erection is. You can learn to recognize feelings of arousal internally or emotionally without having to look at your erection. For women, it is important to get in touch with the strengths and depths your arousal can reach.

The Exercise Start with a genital caress of yourself. As you slowly stroke and explore your genitals, give numbers to the different states of arousal you feel. Caress yourself for about twenty minutes, and every five minutes or so ask yourself, "Where am I now?" Don't try to reach any particular level of arousal. Focus, relax, and breathe. If you get distracted, bring your mind back to your touch. Repeat this exercise until you are able to reliably experience arousal levels of six or seven. Then try the next exercise.

♀ Exercise ♂
Peaking

In this exercise you do a genital caress and bring your arousal up to a peak, and then let it subside.

The Exercise   To begin, relax, breathe, and caress yourself as you did in the previous exercise. When you feel yourself hit level four, stop caressing and allow it to go down one or two levels. Then slowly begin the caress again, and this time let your arousal climb to level five. Stop and let your arousal subside again. Continue this exercise for about twenty minutes or until you reach orgasm. Spend about five minutes per peak, including both the up and down phase.

♀ Exercise ♂
Plateauing

In the peaking exercise you allowed your arousal to go up and down in a wave-like pattern. Plateauing is similar, but here you attempt to ride each arousal level for a few seconds.

There are four techniques you can use to plateau: squeezing your PC muscle, breathing, changing your movements, and changing your focus. In this exercise, you try one technique at each plateau. By practicing these techniques they will become second nature, and in future exercises you can use all of them at once without thinking about it.

The Exercise   Begin a genital caress. When you reach level five, slow down your breathing so that you retreat back to level four.

Then speed up your breathing so that you reach level six. At level six, squeeze your PC muscle a few times until your arousal lowers to level five.

Do sensuous pelvic thrusts against your hand until you reach level seven. At level seven, stop thrusting and allow your arousal to go back to level six.

Now caress yourself again until you reach level eight. Shift your focus, so that although you are still touching yourself, you are focusing on the feelings of another part of your body that you are not touching. You will go back down to level six. Now caress yourself again and see if you can reach level nine.

Can you see how this works? By changing your breathing, your PC muscle squeezing, your thrusting, and your focus, you are able to maintain your arousal at a particular level for anywhere from a few seconds up to a couple of minutes. If at the end of this plateauing exercise you are aroused enough, let yourself fall into the waves of orgasmic release.

Arousal awareness, peaking, and plateauing will help restore your libido. You will feel energy build and discharge if you reach orgasm. I believe that even if you don't climax, the peaking process helps your body produce and release endorphins. The wave-like arousal pattern continued for about twenty minutes will allow endorphins to be released in the most efficient—and pleasurable—way.

Embracing Emotions

Too often people approach sex as a one-way emotional street. We may be insecure in ourselves or have a restricted understanding of appropriate sexual expression. Some people use sex like a drug, to create certain emotions—sex addicts, for example, use sex to relieve anxiety in an unhealthy way. Other people wait until they feel a certain emotion in order to have sex—they must feel in love or lovable to enter a sexual realm. But sex, when it is lovemaking, is a rich and multicolored emotional experience. It both touches and expresses our emotional tapestry.

I think most of us could stand to be more aware of our emotions and be more honest about them when we make love. There is nothing wrong with using sex to explore your emotions, to say "I feel so angry tonight—I want to make love," or to desire to make love at apparently unusual times. Instead of putting your emotions on hold during sex, recognize that sex can be used to convey a multitude of emotions. If you use lovemaking to convey your existing emotions, you can often break down an emotional barrier and release energy. You may find this causes uncontrollable weeping or laughing after sex, but it is nothing to worry about. Releasing those emotions while you are with your partner is potent and positive. I often say, if you work your emotions out during lovemaking *with* your partner, you don't have to work them out later *on* your partner.

Sharpening Mental Abilities

Do you want to improve your mental capacities? Do you wish for a sharper memory, longer attention span, or deeper ability to concentrate? The basic sensate focus process should help, since it is a mental device that improves your focus. If after those exercises you want more help, try the more advanced, sensate focus exercise below.

♀ Exercise ♂
Switching Focus by Yourself

There are a number of things you can focus on during sexual activity. A lot of people focus only on their genitals but there is so much more. There are sights, smells, and sounds. An analogy is listening to an orchestra. Most of us probably hear the composition as a whole, but with more listening experience you will be able to pick out the different orchestra sections and even individual instruments. Another analogy: if you are an experienced cook (or, I suppose, an experienced eater) you will be able to pick out subtle flavors in foods that the rest of us philistines would not recognize.

The Exercise To learn to switch focus, lie comfortably on your bed and begin to caress some part of your body—let's say it is your thigh. Be aware that you can be conscious of your hand touching your thigh or your thigh being touched by your hand. As you focus on sensations, see if you can switch your focus from how your hand feels to how your thigh feels and back again. This one takes a little practice—don't expect to get it the first time. When you master this technique, try doing a genital caress, in which you focus on your hand touching your genitals, and switch to your genitals being touched by your hand. Practice consciously switching your focus back and forth as you continue the genital caress for fifteen or twenty minutes.

Healing Your Attitudes

Attitudes are mental evaluations. We judge things as either positive or negative. Learned ways of thinking that may create problems in lovemaking include: You may have a negative attitude about your body or your partner's body, or about yourself in general or your partner in general. You may have a general negative outlook on the world, expressed in hostility, pessimism, or a chip on the shoulder. Or you may have attitude problems from constantly comparing yourself with other people in terms of physical appearance or success.

Here are two very powerful exercises for developing a stronger, healthier body image.

♀ Exercise ♂
Body Image (Nonverbal)

I'd like to spend some time delving into the issues surrounding body love and body image, because it is an area where many of us need healing. To experience sexual healing it is essential you develop a self-loving, comfortable relationship with your body and physical appearance.

The body image exercise does not involve sensate focus. It is a communication exercise, a process used to help each person become more comfortable with his or her own body and with their partner's body. In this exercise you examine your nude body in detail in front of your partner, and tell your partner what you like and dislike about it. You also discuss whether certain parts of your body have positive or negative feelings associated with them.

Before You Begin   Do this exercise in a well-lit room with a large mirror, preferably full-length. If you can, also have a hand-held mirror.

The Exercise   First, take off your clothing and stand in front of each other, about three feet apart. Gaze into each other's eyes for a minute. Then slowly take in your partner's facial features. Appreciate things you have never noticed before or things you haven't taken the time to notice in a while. Think of your gaze as a sensate focus caress in which you use your eyes instead of your hands. Then, mutually shift your gaze down, over the chest, abdomen, and legs. Let your eyes move slowly over your partner's body, as if you were caressing him or her; take your time and gaze at each part of his or her body for as long as it takes to visually enjoy it. Take time to gaze at each other's genitals. Each of you turns around so that the other person can look at your other side.

Even if you have seen each other without clothing countless times, it may not be acceptable in your relationship to stare at certain body parts, such as breasts or genitals. Or you may not feel comfortable nude. Maybe you are in the habit of wearing sleepwear to bed, or all your sexual activity takes place with the lights off. Partners may not be in the habit of walking around the house nude because of the presence of other family members. For whatever reason, you may not have much experience seeing your partner nude or being seen in the nude, so nudity itself may cause anxiety. If you feel anxious or self-conscious during this part of the exercise, take some deep breaths and express the fact that you feel anxious to your partner.

Men and women have different anxieties about their bodies and about being nude in front of a partner. For men, there are two common beliefs that cause anxiety in this situation: feeling that their penis is too small, and wondering whether they will have an erection. Every male client I have worked with has expressed concern during this exercise that his penis was not large enough. Most men have differing ideas about having an erection when they are naked with a woman. Some expect to have an erection immediately, others allow themselves only one to five minutes. Still others think they should not have an erection at all, and are embarrassed if they do have one. Any and all reactions are individual and normal. This body image exercise is not meant to be a sexual exercise, so if you don't have an erection, that is okay. If you do have an erection during the exercise, just enjoy it and keep doing the exercise. Don't try to make your erection harder, and don't try to make it go away. It is perfectly normal to either have or not have an erection during this exercise.

Not surprisingly, while men's anxieties tend to be centered around their genitals, women tend to worry about their weight and whether parts of their body are unacceptable to their partner. Most women think their breasts are too small, saggy, or the wrong shape, and that their hips and thighs are too large. Part of this feeling is fed by the unwarranted emphasis our culture places on thinness, idealizing a female body that is quite honestly unattainable for the majority of women. This exercise and the ones that follow will help you see the beauty in your body and accept it more.

If you do feel anxious about whether your partner finds your body attractive, don't be hard on yourself. Accept the fact that you have these feelings for now. Your anxieties and feelings about your body and about your partner's reaction to it are real. This exercise helps you learn to accept negative feelings about your body and not let them get in the way of your sexual enjoyment and romantic intimacy. You will also learn how your partner feels about his or her body. I hope that through this exercise you develop the attitude, "My body is capable of feeling wonderfully good, and I love my body for that. I can have sensual and sexual enjoyment of my body if I accept myself the way I am."

♀ Exercise ♂
Body Image (Verbal)

In this next body-image exercise, one of you is passive while the other is active. You will need a hand-held mirror for this.

The Exercise   Let's say that the woman decides to be active first. She takes a long look at herself in the mirror and describes all the parts of her body, and her feelings associated with each part. The man sits comfortably and watches and listens.

When you are active, look at yourself in the mirror carefully. Use a hand mirror to examine the back of your body, then discuss it with your partner. Start with your hair and say what you like or dislike about it, any good or bad feelings or memories that are associated with it, whether you like to touch it or have it touched, and how it feels.

Now do the same for all your other body parts: eyes, ears, nose, mouth, face, neck, shoulders, back, breasts, chest, arms, hands, stomach, waist, thighs, buttocks, genitals, legs, feet. Also include your height, weight, body hair, and any characteristics such as moles, birthmarks, or scars.

When you are the passive person listening to your partner, you may disagree with her descriptions. As the passive person, you should remain quiet—don't interrupt, make comments, or ask questions. You will exchange feedback at the end of the exercise.

After you have described your body parts, examine your body as a whole. Tell your partner your favorite and least favorite parts. What do you consider your best and worst features? What parts cause you anxiety? What parts do you like to have touched and looked at? What parts don't you like to have touched and looked at, and why? What would you change if you could change anything about your body? What would you like to look like and why?

For each partner, things will come up that you could not have predicted. Touching or stroking the body part can bring up memories. For example, I was doing this exercise once and, as I touched my hair, I realized that although I like long hair, my earliest memories of it are of my mother tugging and pulling it, trying to get the tangles out. I associate my hair looking good with pain and discomfort. To this day, I can't stand going to the beauty salon. Why was this realization important? When I was in a sexual situation, I became highly uncomfortable if my partner stroked my hair or touched it at all. You may find a lot of things like this come up for you.

After you have switched roles and the other person has described his or her body, discuss the following: Did you feel your partner was realistic about his or her body? Why or why not? Be careful not to negate your partner's feelings when you phrase your thoughts. Which part of your partner's body do you especially like? When your partner describes his or her feelings about your body, listen hard. Believe and accept them, even though they may not coincide with yours. Try not to negate what your partner says.

Remember that this is *not* a time for bringing up any negative or critical feelings about your partner, or about your past or current relationship. This is a time to learn how you and your partner feel about your own bodies and to honor yourselves in preparation for learning to touch each other in a new way.

Variation   Do you find this exercise uncomfortable? There are other options for this exercise that can make it easier. You can do the body image exercise by yourself in front of a mirror before you do it with a partner. If you are anxious about appearing completely nude in front of your partner, start with just part of your clothing off. You may find that if you go into a lot of detail on each body part, this exercise will take a long time. Instead, you might want to get together once a day with your partner for fifteen minutes or so for a week, and talk about one body part instead of trying to do the whole body all at once.

———

The body image exercises are not easy, because we don't usually discuss our feelings about our body with other people. Exploring these issues together will build trust between you and your partner. It will give you practice in communicating about feelings. And it will provide information about how your partner feels about his or her body, and by extension, sexuality and lovemaking in general.

Another purpose of the body image exercise is to find out if you and your partner have realistic views of your bodies. As a woman, you may find your body unattractive and think your partner is not telling the truth when he says he likes your breasts or your thighs. If you are a man, you may feel that your penis is inadequate, when in fact your partner likes the way it looks and feels. These feelings about yourself and the way you look are probably not negative enough to stand in the way of doing sensate focus exercises together, but they keep you from realizing your true potential. Problems do arise when a person's body image is either totally unrealistic or so negative that he or she cannot relax enough to enjoy sensual arousal.

Many people with unrealistic body images are good-looking, but their self-esteem is so low that they consider themselves ugly. As a surrogate partner I worked with clients of all levels of relative attractiveness. Not once did I encounter a client physically unattractive enough to have it interfere with our ability to engage in sensate focus exercises. Both attractive and unattractive bodies feel good to touch. Every person has beautiful qualities about them. There is no research that I know of about whether attractive people have more satisfying sex lives than less attractive people, or about whether attractive people are physically and mentally healthier.

However, it is possible that there is some aspect of your appearance you would like to change. There are a number of excellent books and other resources available on skin care, health, exercise, and clothing choice. You are an adult, and you have a high degree of choice about how you look. While physical appearance may be given too much importance in this culture, making yourself look more attractive *can* boost your self-esteem, and that is always worthwhile. For example, I didn't always look like this. I was once overweight, flat-chested, wore glasses, and had bad teeth. Plus, my mother dressed me funny. I made a decision to change, and I feel better about myself for it.

Getting feelings and anxieties about your bodies out in the open can eliminate further negative experiences. You may also learn that your partner's reaction to being touched may have much less to do with the way you touch than with his or her own anxieties about body image or body memories.

A client of mine, *Alex,* did not like to kiss, and this caused problems for him in relationships. In the body-image exercise he revealed that he had been in a car accident and had broken his jaw when he was a teenager. He had to have major reconstructive surgery on his face, and especially his lips. The scars from the surgery were no longer visible but the trauma had stayed with him and made him self-conscious. Alex never told his lovers that kissing created anxieties for him, or why. Thus, the women he had been with had not known why he refused to kiss. They thought he had a problem with them, which made them anxious, and the relationships failed.

Have you or your partner had a traumatic experience that has caused you to feel uncomfortable about your naked body or embarrassed about a certain body part? If the body image exercise does bring up a powerful memory or issue for you, remember that sometimes just getting it out in the open can help to release it. When dealing with any powerful, traumatic memory, such as of physical or sexual abuse, consider getting the assistance of a qualified therapist to deal with the issue completely. If a painful memory comes up for your partner, accept his or her feelings completely and be very supportive.

Other Issues of Attitude

Do you have other attitudes that you believe are standing in the way of a fulfilling relationship with your partner? Common stumbling blocks are negativity, hostility, pessimism, and holding grudges or "carrying a chip on your shoulder." These are considered "toxic" emotions or attitudes; they contribute to physical illness. (In fact, depression, anxiety, and hostility are considered the "toxic triad" that tend to cause psychosomatic illnesses.)

I believe that the sexual healing program in this book can help banish these negative emotions. The only other cure I know for them is the "Four Gs": giving, gratitude, graciousness, and the Golden Rule. If you need a quick attitude boost, do one of these things. Think about somebody who is a lot worse off than you are, realize how well off you are, and then figure out some way to help that person, even in a small way. Show some class by being gracious to someone who isn't being very nice to you. And, before you do something to somebody else, consider how that person will feel. These actions may sound sappy, but trust me, they work. If the person you end up being nicer to is your partner, then so much the better.

Photograph by
Paul Dahlquist

Chapter 7

Becoming a Sexual Healer
—Advanced Exercises

**W**orking through Part One, you have learned the fundamentals of healing touch, emotional connection, sexual fitness, and arousal. These fundamentals will allow you to move successfully through the specific sexual healing exercises and programs that follow.

To unlock the power of advanced, sexually oriented exercises, you need to become comfortable and familiar with the sensate focus caresses in Chapter 2. This is the touch that will heal you and your partner. The bonding exercises in Chapter 3 ensure that you and your partner have laid the intimate emotional foundation to enter fully into sexual healing work, which bypasses sexual defenses. It is also important that you have been doing the sexual fitness exercises in Chapter 4, so that you have the instincts and PC muscle ability to do the beginning sexual healer exercises in Chapter 5. And last, the relaxation and arousal exercises in Chapter 6 show you how to bring these things together in a sexual context without pressure and prime you for working together with your partner. Once you have worked through these you will be ready to put them all together and try some very advanced exercises for sexual arousal and orgasm.

Each of the exercises in this chapter and the following chapters addresses a particular aspect of sexual healing. They are more focused and more intense than the exercises you have done up to this point, especially those with sexual intercourse, so be prepared for the resonance you will feel.

Whenever you do any exercise in the program, be sure to set aside enough time (usually an hour for most exercises) and work in a room with no distractions. It is very important that you take the time to spoon breathe at the beginning of the session, during the role switch, and at the end of the exercise, so that you center yourselves before entering into the exercise and you ground yourselves after it. I'll remind you to do so at the beginning of each exercise description. Make sure you don't skip or skimp on this—you need gentle touching to open yourselves to emotional and sexual connection and transition out of it. Otherwise you may not find yourself able to focus during the exercises or you may feel very vulnerable after them. If the main exercise involves the genitals and intercourse, be sure to do focusing caresses (short back or front caresses) so that you are both relaxed.

The advanced exercises in this chapter are intended to deepen your bond and heal your relationship through the power of sexual arousal. The exercises in this chapter will help you learn and become in tune with your partner's sexual response. You will also learn to be highly aware of your own sexual response, and how to communicate about it in an open, nondemanding, pressure-free way.

Remember, when you are the active partner, touch for your own pleasure. When you are the passive partner, allow yourself to simply enjoy the sensations. These exercises may be advanced, but don't forget the basics of touch: focus, breathe, relax. The only things you should be thinking about when doing these exercises are the basics, and enjoying yourself and loving your partner.

♀ Exercise ♂
Sensuous Oral Sex

After you have done the genital caress with your partner often enough to be comfortable with it, you are ready to explore oral sex.

Sensuous oral sex is another variation on the genital caress. But before I describe the exercise, let me say a few words about oral sex in general.

Many people have either never experienced oral sex or find the practice unappealing. Others perform oral sex and either do not enjoy it, or feel coerced into it, or do it to please the other person. They simply want to get it over with. Oral sex is probably associated with more anxiety than any other sexual practice, including intercourse.

Many sexual self-help books talk about oral sex as though there are techniques you can perform that will guarantee orgasm for your partner, or techniques that every man or every woman will enjoy all the time. This is misleading. Being able to enjoy oral sex—both giving and receiving—depends more on how relaxed and focused you are than it does on any technical prowess.

If you hold negative attitudes toward oral sex, relax. There is nothing inherently gross or dirty about our genitals. If your partner has washed his or her genitals and is free of infection, you have nothing to worry about.

I encourage you to experience oral sex in the context of a sensate focus exercise because there are few things as delightful as giving or receiving a sensuous, pressure-free oral genital caress. You may be surprised to find that when the performance aspect is removed from oral sex, you will like it.

The Exercise for a Man　　Begin caressing your partner with a front caress, then slowly begin stroking her genitals with your hand. Have your partner lie down or sit leaning back with her legs spread apart so you can comfortably put your face between her legs. She can prop her buttocks up with a pillow so your neck does not get sore.

As the active partner, you do an oral caress with your tongue the same way you did a genital caress with your hand. Keep your lips, tongue, chin, and neck as relaxed as you can. Slowly move your tongue along your partner's inner thighs, outer vaginal lips, and inner vaginal lips. Let your tongue glide over her clitoris, and flick in and out of her vagina. You may also want to use your lips.

Focus on the exact point of contact, and explore how the different parts of your partner's genitals feel and taste on the different parts of your mouth. If your tongue, chin, or neck starts to get tired or sore, change positions and relax. You may find yourself holding your tongue too stiffly in order to please your partner.

Don't stiffen your tongue and rub it forcefully against her clitoris. Don't forcefully suck or slurp at her vaginal lips. And don't use your fingers. If you insert a finger into her vagina or rub her clitoris while you lick her vagina, your partner will probably interpret these actions as a demand to respond. Whether or not she is aware of this, she will remain anxious and not be able to relax. The point of the exercise is for you to enjoy the sensations in your mouth and for your partner to be able to relax and enjoy herself—with no demands on her to show how much she likes it.

The Exercise for a Woman   Have your partner sit or lie back in a comfortable position, and spend a few minutes on a front caress. Then gently caress your partner's genitals with your hand for a few minutes until you are both focused and relaxed.

Lower you head to his pelvis and slowly use your tongue and lips to lick all over his thighs and penis and scrotum. Explore freely, and do what makes your tongue feel good. Lick the area behind the testicles. Insert your tongue into the creases between the thighs and scrotum. You may want to take his whole penis in your mouth and slowly let it back out again. Experience how each different area feels and tastes on your lips and tongue.

Don't put pressure on your partner or yourself. Think of your own pleasure, not your partner's. Don't suck on the penis in such a way that your head moves up and down—only your tongue and lips should move during this exercise. If your neck or tongue becomes tired or sore, move into a different position. Your tongue should remain relaxed and not stiff. If you feel pressured to perform, stop and caress some other part of your partner's body until you feel that you are focused enough to enjoy the oral sex again. It is best if you respond to what *you* want, rather than what you think your partner wants.

If your partner indicates that he is about to ejaculate, decide whether to take the semen in your mouth or whether to temporarily stop the caress while your partner ejaculates. If you are not through with the caress, wipe off the semen and continue.

Don't use your hand to masturbate your partner during this caress. Remember, you are doing this caress only for your own pleasure and to heal. It doesn't matter whether your partner gets aroused, has an erection, or ejaculates. What does matter is that you do what feels good for you and that you focus on the sensations in your mouth during the caress.

To recap the sequence: Spoon breathing and focusing caress — Genital caress — Oral caress.

One word of caution to both partners: no biting. No matter how aroused, playful, or comfortable you feel, do not bite your partner's genitals. These are some of the most sensitive tissues in the human body, and if you do anything abrupt or hurtful during this exercise, your partner may never forgive you.

♀ Exercise ♂
Genital Caress with Verbal Feedback

Remember the genital caress you did with your partner in Chapter 5? It was important that that was pressure-free, with no verbal communication. But now, in order to learn more about each other's response, you and your partner may also want to do a version of the genital caress in which you give each other feedback about the types of touching you enjoy on your genitals.

The Exercise   Begin by doing a sensuous genital caress with either manual or oral stimulation or both. When you are the passive partner, at the end of the caress tell your partner one or two things that he or she did that you found particularly pleasurable. Be specific. Then ask your partner to do those things again.

Allow yourself to enjoy what you asked for for several minutes. If it is not exactly what you wanted, gently guide your partner's hand or face and give him or her more feedback until the caress is exactly the way it pleases you. Then tell your partner something that he or she didn't do, but that you would like. You may take your partner's hand and gently guide it to receive what you want for a few minutes.

Here's the sequence: Focusing caress — Genital caress and/or oral caress — Passive partner says what is pleasurable, asks for more, gives guidance.

♀ Exercise ♂
Peaking with Your Partner

In Chapter 6, you learned how to peak at high arousal levels by yourself. As I have explained earlier, I believe peaking and prolonged states of arousal are very important, because this wave-like arousal pattern brings about optimal, continued release of endorphins. Both peaking and plateauing (the exercise that follows) intensify orgasm. Peaking and plateauing with a lover can be a dynamic, passionate experience.

The Exercise   Let's begin with the woman active and the man passive. The man lies on his back, while the woman begins a front caress and a genital caress. As his arousal climbs, the man tells her the levels it hits. For example, the woman asks, "Tell me when you reach level four" and when he says "Four," she stops the caress and allows his arousal to decrease a couple of levels.

This is just like peaking by yourself, only now you are completely passive, savoring your partner's touch and communicating your arousal to her. Let your arousal peak up the scale with manual and oral stimulation for as long as you like, peaking at levels five, six, seven, eight, nine, and ten, if you can. Then switch roles.

You will learn about your partner's arousal cycle by paying attention to his or her breathing and heartbeat. Feel the heat that emanates from your partner's skin as his or her arousal heightens. When you end your role as the active partner in the exercise, lightly place your hand or face on your partner's heart and listen.

Here's the sequence again: Focusing caresses and genital caresses — Passive partner peaks as active partner caresses, stops, caresses — Passive partner says arousal levels aloud.

♀ Exercise ♂
Plateauing with Your Partner

Remember (from Chapter 6) that plateauing is very similar to peaking, but here the focus is on maintaining a certain level of arousal. There are four ways to plateau your arousal: changing your breathing, changing your focus, using your PC muscle, and changing your movements.

The Exercise   Let's have the man be active first. His partner lies on her back while he does a front and genital caress to stir her arousal.

When you are passive, accept your partner's delicate touch. As you reach level four on the arousal scale, try to stay there for a few seconds by slowing your breathing. If you go beyond a four, slow your breathing down until you are back at four. If you go below level four, speed up your breathing until you are slightly past level four. This takes intense concentration on both your own responses and the stimulation your partner provides for you.

For your next plateau, try to maintain your arousal level by doing pelvic rolls or thrusts. Your partner continues to caress your genitals, either manually or orally. If you have decided to plateau at level six, start some sensuous pelvic movements around level four. Then speed up the movements until you reach level six. If you go beyond six, slow your thrusting down until you are below a six. Then speed up rolls and thrusts to allow your arousal to climb to six again.

Try the next plateau—seven or eight—by using your PC muscle to take your arousal down and pelvic rolls and thrusts to bring it back up. Soon you will be able to maintain your arousal level within a narrow range that you can control. You will be able to recognize very subtle changes in your arousal level such as five-and-a-half, six-and-a-half, and seven-and-a-half.

For your last plateau, try one in which you switch your focus from one part of your body to another. For example, try to plateau at level eight. If you go beyond eight, mentally switch your focus from the part of your genitals that your partner is caressing to some other part. This will lower your arousal level slightly. Then switch your focus back to the area being touched in order to move back up to eight. If you feel like having an orgasm, let yourself fall into one, but don't pressure yourself. Then switch roles and have your partner practice plateauing using the four techniques. Pretty soon you will both be able to use all the techniques at each plateau without having to think about them.

Here's the sequence again: Focusing caresses — Passive partner plateaus as active partner caresses without stopping — Plateaus with breathing, then pelvic movements, then PC muscle, then switching focus.

♀ Exercise ♂
Asking for What You Want

Many people feel that sexual expression comes naturally, and thus sexual pleasure should come naturally as well. While this may be the case for some lucky few, most people have greater satisfaction—and intimacy—in their sexual relationship when they share more specific communications with their partner. "Asking for What You Want" is a communication exercise that helps you feel comfortable asking for what you want in a pressure-free way. Be careful what you ask for—you'll get it, so enjoy it!

The Exercise   This exercise begins the minute you enter the room. Mutually decide who will be active first. Let's say in this case it is the man.

From the moment he enters the room, he asks for anything he wants. Nothing in the exercise will happen until he requests it. If he wants his partner to be naked, he must say, "Please take off your clothes." If he wishes his partner to remove his clothes, he must say, "Please take off my clothes." And so on. Make sure you tell your partner everything that you want her to do. You may ask for anything you can think of that you would like your partner to do, but you do need to be specific.

At this stage of the program, only ask for things that you have already done together, and ask your partner for things you both are comfortable with. If you repeat the exercise later you can ask for more. If what your partner does is not exactly what you desire, say so kindly and give her directions until she gets it right. Feel free to enjoy whatever you have asked your partner to do for as long as you want.

When active, you may also do whatever you like, as long as you tell your partner what you are going to do beforehand. For example, if you would like to touch her for a while, you could say, "I want you to lie down so I can caress your back for a while."

When you are the passive partner in this exercise, simply do as your partner asks. Don't worry; you will have your turn. Refuse only if your partner asks you to do something that is painful or unpleasant. Much as you might want to initiate something, don't—unless your partner requests it. See if you can actually do what he asks you to, but do it for your own enjoyment and focus on it. The secret is to accommodate your partner's wishes while still doing the activities for yourself.

This exercise can be awkward for some people because they are not used to asking for what they want. When you are the asker, be assertive and don't settle for something that is not exactly what you desire. Make your requests clear. For example, rather than saying, "Would you like to give me a front caress?" or, "You wouldn't want to give me a front caress, would you?", say "Please give me a front caress" or, "I'd like you to give me a front caress."

When you are the askee, accommodate your partner's wishes but do everything for your own pleasure as much as possible by focusing on your own sensual enjoyment. If you feel uncomfortable doing something your partner asks for, just say "No."

If your partner says no to some activity you request, it doesn't mean, "No, never, that's disgusting." It simply means "No, I do not want to do that particular activity right now."

You can do this exercise with each person in the active role for half an hour. The exercise can be stressful, but it can also pinpoint problems you may be having in asserting or enjoying yourself. Were you paralyzed by thoughts such as "I wanted to ask for such and such but I didn't think you'd want to do it?" Did you feel on an equal footing? Did you have difficulties explaining what you wanted? If you had these or other thoughts, share them with your partner and try the exercise again later.

The major benefit you will receive from this exercise is that you will learn to ask your partner for something sensual or sexual in a healthy, pressure-free way. You and your partner will gradually learn to overcome second-guessing in your sexual communication.

Have you had fun with these exercises? Do you and your partner feel emboldened and adventurous? Are you ready to try some sexual healing exercises that include intercourse? Read on.

Photograph by Craig Morey

Chapter 8

How to Be a Sexual Healer with Intercourse

ow it is time to come together in the ultimate healing connection—intercourse. "Intercourse" means communication; it expresses a deep connection between two partners as well as different intentions. This chapter will show you many ways to have intercourse with different healing mindsets and different healing goals. The peaking and plateauing techniques you learned in Chapters 6 and 7 will amplify your feelings during the following exercises.

Although what follows contains short descriptions of different ways to have intercourse, these are not different positions, as you would find in a typical sex manual. When you have intercourse, use whichever positions are comfortable for the two of you. The suggestions I make are simply that, suggestions. They are based on my experience and the positions that seem to best convey healing.

Before you try any of these exercises, it is very important that you have spent time spoon breathing and caressing each other with nonsexual and sexual caresses. You may also wish to spend time with oral caresses and sensuous oral sex. This time is needed to get centered within yourself, relax and focus on your arousal, and get in sync with your partner. After intercourse, maintain physical contact and take time to spoon breathe together or nurture each other in an embrace. You will need a "coming down" period to re-ground yourselves after the experiences of healing intercourse.

If you decide to have intercourse after doing another, non-intercourse exercise, remember your basics. Relax and enter the healing mindset. Allow time, so you do not feel rushed. And get centered together by beginning with spoon breathing, focusing caresses, and genital caresses.

♀ Exercise ♂
Goal-Free Intercourse

The theory behind goal-free intercourse is to escape the pressure to have, or to give, an orgasm. Intercourse without orgasm nurtures the mindset of continuity between skin sensuality, foreplay, and intercourse. As you enjoy goal-free intercourse, you learn to be more flexible and indulgent in your lovemaking, and to not think of intercourse as the result of foreplay, or of orgasm as the necessary end result of intercourse.

The Exercise Decide who will be active and who will be passive. When the woman is active, she begins by doing a sensate focus caress on her partner—front, genital, and oral. When he gets an erection, she climbs onto him and makes slow, sensuous strokes, as many as she desires. He remains passive and doesn't move; his only responsibility is to focus on the pleasurable sensations.

There should be no performance pressure, no goals, no thinking ahead, and no orgasm. After this short exercise, the woman maintains the sexual connection by lowering herself into an embrace with her partner.

When the man is active, the woman lies on her back. Her only responsibility is to focus on her own sensations. Her partner does a front caress, and genital and oral caresses. He can kneel and use his penis to caress the outside of her vagina if this arouses him. When he is ready for intercourse, he can put a pillow underneath her, raise her legs, and enter her. This position, in which the woman raises her legs and the man kneels between them, brings them into a lovely face-to-face connection and offers greater stimulation for both. (If you have trouble kneeling, you can also use the missionary position.) The man does a few slow, sensuous strokes, as he desires, and when finished, lies lovingly on top of or beside his partner.

♀ Exercise ♂
Sensate Focus Intercourse

This is intercourse with a different focus—sensuality. In previous chapters you have practiced focusing on skin sensations in all parts of the body. Now you will learn to focus on the specific, erotic sensations of the penis in the vagina.

The Exercise with the Man Active   Ask your partner to lie comfortably on her back, and do sensuous caresses, including a front caress, a genital caress, or an oral-genital caress. If you need direct stimulation to have an erection, use your penis to caress your partner's vagina, or caress yourself with your hand.

When you are ready, start intercourse in the kneeling position (described in the exercise above). As the active partner, you will control the speed of thrusting. Thrust as slowly as possible—try to caress your partner's vagina with your penis. Both of you should feel free to move, to thrust and roll with each other, while focusing on the exquisite sensations of your penis inside her vagina.

Next, try switching your focus from penis to vagina to different parts of the penis. What can you feel? Both of you focus on the same sensations at the same time. Look at each other as you focus. There should be no pressure for either of you to have an orgasm, but if you do that is okay. As the active partner, you decide when intercourse is over.

The Exercise with the Woman Active   Ask your partner to lie on his back as you do a front caress, a genital caress, and perhaps oral sex. When he has an erection, climb on top and begin slowly thrusting on his penis. Think of caressing it with your vagina. Both of you should focus on the sensations of his penis inside your vagina.

As the active partner, you lead in the speed and extent of thrusting, and your partner follows. It's like dancing—in fact it *is* a dance, a love dance. As you make love, look into each other's eyes and try to match your breathing. The exercise is over whenever you decide to stop, regardless of whether either or both of you has an orgasm.

♀ Exercise ♂
Healing Intercourse

This is also intercourse freed from pressure or goals. In healing intercourse, you visualize and project healing sexual energy in a focused way.

The Exercise with the Woman Active Caress your partner while you both center your energies together. When he has a partial or full erection, climb on top and begin intercourse. While thrusting and focusing, visualize your vagina as a vessel that surrounds your partner's penis. Imagine your vagina is hot, giving out a white, healing light that flows into your partner.

This visualization will convey a positive healing energy from your vagina to your partner's penis. If your partner focuses on the same visualization, your vagina will actually begin to feel hot during this exercise.

There is no goal, no pressure, and no time limit. You decide when the exercise is over. If you are able to reach a climax, give him the ultimate healing energy gift—you having a very intense orgasm.

The Exercise with the Man Active Begin with a front caress, genital caress, and perhaps oral sex. When your partner is aroused and lubricated, begin intercourse in the kneeling position. Visualize your penis as a healing instrument, radiating white-hot, healing energy to your partner. Or think of your sexual energy as a blue or white light flowing into your partner. Both of your should focus on the visualization. You can continue with intercourse as long as you want to, with or without an orgasm. You may actually feel your penis become hot.

Sometimes it is easier for a man to do this visualization because, if he has an orgasm, he actually is pouring something into his partner. So if you are a woman, when you have an orgasm, picture it as an energy gift—powerful, hot, and healing.

♀ Exercise ♂
Heart Awareness Intercourse

This form of intercourse creates an incredible bond, especially if one or both of you has an orgasm. During heart awareness intercourse, you listen to your lover's heartbeat as the rhythms of your lovemaking build and climax. This exercise will sharpen your awareness to the rhythms of your bodies, your arousal, and ultimately, each other. Alternatively, you can adjust your position so that your hearts are against each other and beat together as you make love.

Begin the exercise with caresses and intimate bonding.

The Exercise with the Woman Active　　Straddle your partner and thrust sensuously. While making love, lean over and rest your ear on your partner's chest. Feel his warmth. Listen to his heartbeat as you both become more and more aroused. See if you can cause his heartbeat to speed up or slow down with the speed and force of your thrusting. As his heart beats faster, does his breathing quicken? Does your arousal climb? Does your heart beat faster?

The Exercise with the Man Active　　Kneel between your partner's legs and enter your partner. As you slowly and sensuously thrust, lean over so your ear rests on your partner's chest. Feel her warmth and listen to her heartbeat. Does the speed and passion of your thrusting affect the beating of her heart? Does her breathing quicken? Does your arousal climb in tandem?

———

Now, here are some intercourse exercises intended to deepen and enrich arousal. They teach you to peak and plateau during intercourse, while you take turns being active. Realizing the potential of your arousal unleashes lots of sexual energy, and fosters a strong sense of mutuality. I hope you will find new pleasure and passion with these.

♀ Exercise ♂
Peaking with Intercourse

There are several ways to do this, depending on which of you is active and who is on top. I will describe four different options. Keep in mind that it doesn't matter how highly aroused you get in any exercise. With mutual agreement you can always stop the exercise and have regular intercourse or exchange loving caresses. Orgasm is not the goal, though it will be delicious if you go there.

The time frame on all these peaking exercises is about twenty minutes, give or take a few. During a twenty-minute exercise, most people are comfortable doing about five peaks and taking about four minutes for the up and down phases of the peak. Depending on your personal response style, you can compress the peaks or lengthen them. Do what feels comfortable and pleasing. Twenty to twenty-five minutes of peaking seems to be about right for optimal endorphin release.

During the peaking exercises, both of you should visualize or feel the peaks as waves. At first you may not peak together, but with time you will become so in tune with each other's bodies and your arousal that your arousal will develop mutually and build upon each other's. Together you may reach new heights.

Man on Top, Man Peaking   Start intercourse in a kneeling position. Let your partner know when you reach level-four arousal. Then stop, or slow down. Do this not to keep from ejaculating but to create the energy wave that releases endorphins. Try peaking at levels five, six, seven, eight, and nine. If your partner is able to follow the peaks with you, that's great. With practice she will learn to read your body and intuit your arousal, so there will be no need to say the numbers out loud. If you have an orgasm during this exercise, I guarantee it will be explosive.

Man on Top, Woman Peaking   Start intercourse in a kneeling position, but this time your partner gives the feedback. She tells you when she's at level-four arousal, and then you slow down. She will signal you to start again with a light touch on your back. Let her peak at levels five, six, seven, eight, and nine. Can you follow her up to the point that you orgasm together? With practice, you will be able to.

Woman on Top, Woman Peaking   Start intercourse astride your partner. Thrust until you reach level-four arousal, then let your partner know. Slow down, and control all your own peaks from level four up through level ten, if you can reach it.

Woman on Top, Man Peaking   Start intercourse as before, but this time your partner gives the feedback at levels four, five, six, seven, eight, and nine. Stop and start or slow your movements to accommodate him. He can speak or lightly touch your back to let you know the levels of his arousal. Keep your thrusting sensuous and slow, and both of you will feel every burning stroke.

♀ Exercise ♂
Plateauing with Intercourse

Plateauing with intercourse is a more challenging adventure. Remember that when you plateau, you coast at a particular arousal level for a few seconds up to a few minutes maximum. Plateauing, especially at very high arousal levels, can give you maximum endorphin release and create an altered state of consciousness. At these high levels of arousal you may experience a distortion of time, so that plateaus that last a few seconds seem to last longer.

Remember also that there are four techniques you can use to maintain a plateau: the PC muscle squeeze, breathing, pelvic movements, and shifting focus. The one you make the most use of in the following exercises is breathing.

Man on Top, Man Plateauing Start intercourse in a kneeling position, and peak at levels four, five and six. Then plateau at level seven, go over to seven-and-a-half, slow down your movements and breathing and slip back to level six-and-a-half.

Then speed up your breathing, hover there for several seconds, and plateau at level eight or nine. At this stage your breathing will almost be panting, your sensations will be very intense, and you will feel as if you are almost hyperventilating to stay on the edge. At orgasm, open your eyes wide and take a deep breath.

Man on Top, Woman Plateauing After you start intercourse, your partner will let you know as she peaks at levels four, five, and six. Based on her feedback, slow down or speed up your movements. She will control her plateaus at levels seven, eight, and nine by alternately slowing her breathing and panting. She can also hover at certain plateaus by changing her pelvic movements or squeezing her PC muscle.

Woman on Top, Woman Plateauing   In this version of the exercise, the woman uses her partner's penis to pleasure herself. Sensuously stroke yourself and thrust up and down to build your arousal. Peak and plateau by controlling the speed of your movements and your breathing. See if you can hover at levels seven, eight, and nine for up to a minute. If you orgasm, open your eyes wide and take a deep breath.

Woman on Top, Man Plateauing   After you start intercourse, your partner will give you feedback when he reaches peaks and plateaus. He will control his plateaus at levels seven, eight, and nine by alternately slowing his breathing and panting. He can also hover at certain plateaus by changing his pelvic movements or squeezing his PC muscle.

♀ Exercise ♂
Mutuality Intercourse

For this exercise, you can have intercourse in whatever position you choose. The idea is to try to see and feel the intercourse from the viewpoint of your partner. In doing so you will find that you cannot tell where you end and your partner begins. You will feel ultimately unified, a greater whole than each of you individually.

The Exercise   There are two ways to experience mutual intercourse. The first is to begin with peaking first, so you are at higher arousal levels when you start intercourse. As you penetrate, ask yourself, "Is what I feel the penis or the vagina?" If you are a woman, see if you can put your consciousness in your partner's penis. If you are a man, see if you can put your consciousness in your partner's vagina.

The second way to experience mutuality is to pretend your positions are reversed. If you are on top, close your eyes and imagine you are on the bottom. If you are on the bottom, close your eyes and imagine you are on top. As you have intercourse and you both mutually focus on this sensation, you feel the sensation that the two of you are spinning or whirling through space.

A third option is to try to place your consciousness in the body of your partner and try to focus on what the intercourse feels like for him or her.

How do you feel about the powers of sexual healing now that you've shared healing intercourse? Did you find that some of these approaches resonate with you and your partner more than others? You may wish to incorporate aspects of them into your general lovemaking as well. Be aware as you incorporate healing intercourse into your love life that you don't develop a performance attitude or lose touch with your partner's needs. Let the power of healing intercourse truly deepen and enrich your relationship, especially as you move on to the specific aspects of healing in the next chapters.

*Photograph by
Paul Dahlquist*

Chapter 9

Lovemaking to Heal
Physical Ailments

believe very strongly in the healing power of love-making because I've witnessed some incredible physical healing take place in my surrogate work. I believe that if this type of healing can develop between a client and a surrogate partner, then the intimate bond of lovers—the physical, emotional, mental, and spiritual mutuality you share with your partner—can be even stronger. And researchers are only now realizing how strong this power can be. The media has begun reporting increasing instances of spontaneous healing and spontaneous remission. In the introduction, you read about some people's experiences of sexual healing, and you will read about others' in this chapter. If unbelievable outcomes like these occur spontaneously, imagine the power you can create when you *intend* to heal yourself and your partner.

Put simply, the information in this chapter is ground-breaking. Many people abstractly believe that lovemaking can positively affect physical illness, but here for the first time is a specific, self-help program that will show you how. First, I describe physical ailments and explain categories for treating them. From there, I discuss the concepts of mind-body healing and how sexual union, specifically, nourishes the mind-body connection. I offer specific strategies for healing different types of physical conditions. At the end of the chapter I have included general exercises that are rewarding if you have physical limitations. Throughout, you will find personal stories from my practice. By reflecting on the healing experiences described in them, you might find insight into your own.

What Is Illness?

When approaching physical illness from the perspective of healing, I treat four areas of illness: psychosomatic illnesses, stress disorders, chronic illnesses, and physical conditions that result from trauma. As a surrogate partner and therapist, these categories serve me well when developing healing approaches and designing programs for clients. By understanding the root cause of an illness, you can emphasize exercises that address that cause as well as the symptoms. Like many aspects of our health, there may be overlap between these categories.

Psychosomatic Illnesses   I talked a bit about psychosomatic illnesses in Chapter 1 when introducing the mind-body relationship, but would like to explain more here. Contrary to popular belief, a psychosomatic illness is not "all in your head." While psychology plays a part in creating or maintaining a psychosomatic illness, both the pain and the tissue damage are real. I believe most illnesses have a psychosomatic component, and can be partially healed psychologically. I have seen even serious medical conditions such as cancer respond to psychological intervention. When medical professionals talk about psychosomatic illnesses, they usually refer to specific conditions, including cardiovascular problems; ulcers and other gastrointestinal problems; asthma; skin problems such as psoriasis; immune disorders such as arthritis; chronic pain; migraines; and menstrual problems.

Stress Disorders   Psychologists usually call stress disorders "psychological factors affecting physical conditions." This category includes any medical problem in which stress plays a role. Stress grows out of the necessity to adjust to changes in one's environment. So stress-related disorders include psychosomatic illnesses as well as more vague conditions such as fatigue, and short-term conditions such as heartburn or neck pain.

When you experience long-term stress, your adrenal glands secrete hormones that degrade your organs over time. In some cases, people have dropped dead from a major stressor. The difference between psychosomatic illnesses and stress disorders is the *cause* of the ailment, not the actual physical symptoms. Stress disorders are caused by environmental factors, whereas psychosomatic illnesses are generally caused by long-term anxiety or depression.

Chronic Illnesses   I consider chronic illnesses to be ongoing, incurable, and usually degenerative conditions that a person copes with on a daily basis. For example, lupus, diabetes, multiple sclerosis, Parkinson's disease, cancer, Huntington's disease, and amyotrophic lateral sclerosis (ALS) are considered chronic illnesses. Sexual healing can help alleviate the discomforts of chronic illness, strengthen the immune system, and feed a person's overall well-being—a key to living successfully with chronic illness.

Physical Trauma   In this category I include conditions resulting from accidents and surgery, such as spinal cord injury, major burns, cerebral palsy, and limb amputation. I also include severe obesity and genetic defects here, because many issues are the same. Conditions resulting from physical trauma are most likely to be considered disfiguring, and so call on special elements of sexual healing. In our culture, physical attraction can be a big part of sexual attraction, and conditions in which a person looks different requires healing issues of self-acceptance and self-worth. If you are the partner of someone with a condition resulting from physical trauma, sexual healing can also heal issues or attitudes you have about health and physical appearance, and how they relate—or don't relate—to making love.

The sexual healing of physical ailments draws on the holistic power of an individual's mental and physical self. However, there are types of illness that, because of their causes, cannot benefit from the power of sexual healing, and so I do not include them in physical healing programs. They include schizophrenia, severe clinical depression, multiple personality disorder, and dementia, such as Alzheimer's disease. These illnesses have mental causes and require specific, professional mental health intervention. If you or your partner exhibits symptoms of these ailments, you should seek professional help.

Somatoform Disorders

Somatoform disorders are mental problems that mimic physical conditions. "Somatoform" comes from the Greek word for body, *soma*, and means "body-like." The most common somatoform disorders are hypochondria and somatization disorder. Hypochondria is typified by obsession with the idea that one has a physical illness, and people with hypochondria typically exaggerate symptoms and "doctor-shop." A person with hypochondria shows no evidence of tissue damage or cause of illness. A person with somatization disorder, on the other hand, describes various symptoms in many of the body's systems. Again, a person will experience symptoms of ailments, but show no apparent tissue damage or physical cause.

I include these explanations here because I have found that psychosomatic illnesses are highly treatable through lovemaking. But somatoform disorders, because they are not physical illnesses, require some form of mental health intervention.

Mind-Body Concepts

Before we delve into healing techniques for medical conditions, there are several valuable concepts in mind-body medicine that you should understand. Somatopsychics and the "placebo effect" exemplify the power of mind-body interaction and suggest ways we can draw on its healing potential.

Somatopsychology

It is true: the mind affects the body. This is the simple basis of the techniques in *Sexual Healing*. But an often-overlooked corollary is that the body also affects the mind. The study of how changes in the body affect the mind is called somatopsychology. Remember the basics of this idea from Chapter 6? By physically moving our body into certain positions or by performing certain physical activities, we can influence our psychological states, particularly our moods. Because the mind-body relationship is a two-way street, body work, massage, and other types of somatopsychic treatment are very important for people with physical illnesses.

There are many different types of massage, which are used for different purposes. By now you have experienced how sensate focus or sensual massage can bring about sexual healing and alleviate emotional problems. Well-known massage techniques, such as Swedish massage, are used for treating sore muscles and inducing relaxation. There are also a number of lesser-known types of massage that are used to increase both physical and mental well-being. They work by simultaneously easing tension out of the body and bringing up repressed emotions.

In addition to sensate focus, you may want to try other types of massage to work out specific physical problems or unconscious conflicts. Here is a list of somatopsychic massage techniques, adapted from *From Acupressure to Zen* by Barbara Nash.

- Feldenkrais—hands-on movements and a series of slow floor exercises to retrain the central nervous system and improve body functioning, awareness, and self-image.

- Rolfing—a type of deep-tissue massage and manipulation that "untangles" the connective tissues and restructures the skeletal system to get rid of tension.

- Bioenergetics—use of specific physical movements to work out chronically tense muscles and deepen contact with the body.

- Tragerwork—gentle movement of muscles and joints to promote relaxation and playfulness.

- Shiatsu—finger pressure on specific areas of the body to release tension and increase circulation of vital energy.

- Polarity Therapy—a system of massage, awareness skills, nutrition, and stretching exercises to balance the energies of the body.

In the introduction I told the story of *Marsha,* who found that receiving a massage brought up undisclosed material about being molested as a girl. Massage, especially in the pelvic region, can help access repressed sexual material. The sensate focus exercises that you will do in this program, because of their sexual nature, are even more likely than nonsexual massage to help you get in touch with repressed and early memories.

The Placebo Effect

The placebo effect is often brought up in a negative context, but in fact it is a testament to the power of our minds. A placebo is a sugar pill, or "fake" pill, used in medical research. The placebo effect refers to how a medication often works if you believe it will, even if it is composed of an ineffective substance. The placebo effect comes about from your positive expectation that your health will improve.

Expectations are crucial in health care, and negative expectations are just as important as positive expectations. For example, if you were ill and visited a doctor who said, "You know, you're probably not going to get better," or "You might as well try this—

it *might* work," wouldn't you change doctors? Physicians provide treatment, often in the form of medication, for specific physical problems; but the major reasons people visit physicians are psychological: stress, fatigue, anxiety, or depression. We really seek a physician's care to have another person convey a positive expectation that we will get better. Do you feel better right after you *make* the doctor's appointment? It's the placebo effect. Your immune system receives a huge temporary boost from your body when your mind knows you've done something to help yourself heal.

The placebo effect also works through touch. The "laying on of hands" has been a common treatment throughout history and in many cultures. In contemporary society, physicians and other health-care givers who touch their patients promote healing because they convey nonverbally the expectation that the patient will get well.

The placebo effect occurs not only in health care, and not just in response to touch. The power of positive expectations in educational settings, the workplace, and in personal relationships has been documented in many studies. Harnessing this power is the subject of many books, seminars, and trainings today.

Understanding the mind-body phenomenon and the nature of psychosomatic illness is important because, if you want to heal yourself or your partner of physical ailments, you will need to learn to convey that sense of positive expectations. By imbuing your touch and sexual activities with positive, healthful expectations, you will make the most of the healing mindset you learned about in the introduction.

Sexual Healing of Psychosomatic Illnesses

Why can psychosomatic illnesses be healed through lovemaking? For the most part because anxiety and depression, the root causes of these ailments, are mediators between sex and physical problems. By enhancing sex we can dissipate anxiety and depression and alleviate physical symptoms. (For more specific ways to get rid of anxiety and depression, see Chapter 6.) Sex can also heal psychosomatic illnesses because touch activates the parasympathetic nervous system (PNS), which mediates relaxation, and deactivates the adrenaline-based sympathetic nervous system (SNS). Touch also releases a flow of endorphins—the pleasurable, pain-relieving brain chemicals. And touching specific areas moves blood flow, the purveyor of our body's sustenance, to those areas.

Any general exercises that you select from this book will have beneficial effects on psychosomatic conditions. When working with clients, I recommend the following program for all psychosomatic conditions. It combines exercises to do alone and to do with your partner.

Begin by working through the self-touch exercises in Chapter 2 and the relationship-bonding exercises in Chapter 3. These will open the channels of your mind-body connection and introduce the healing nature of your loving relationship. Use the sexual fitness exercises in Chapter 4 to tone your PC muscle and learn to relax your other pelvic muscles. The beginning sexual healing exercises in Chapter 5 will help focus your sexual awareness, and the relaxation and breathing exercises on pages 84 and 85 can be used anytime to bring out your healing energies.

Beyond these basics, you can learn to caress yourself and your partner in such a way that you direct blood flow to specific body areas for healing. For each of the following medical conditions, specific touches can have the best benefit.

Cardiovascular Problems   These include angina, chest pain, shortness of breath, high blood pressure, and poor circulation, especially in the lower half of the body. Many men who take high blood pressure medication wish to go off it, because it can affect erections. To help treat high blood pressure, make ample use of the breathing and muscle relaxation exercises. For angina, do the same—you should try to promote relaxation as much as possible. For poor circulation, when you receive a front caress or back caress, have your partner massage *toward* the affected part of your body, literally forcing blood flow from the center of the body to the legs or arms. Although you need to use a stronger massage technique for this stroke, the caress can still be given in a sensual, focused way. I also recommend exploring nurturing and trust-based partner exercises that "open your heart."

If you have a condition that results in a sexual problem, refer to Chapters 10 and 11 on men's and women's specific problems. When you receive the front caress, have your partner massage away from the legs and arms toward the center of the body. And be sure to do all the exercises in which you place your hand or face on your partner's heart; this will strengthen your healing intention and connection.

Breathing Difficulties   These include asthma, allergies, and sinus problems. Many people with asthma are afraid to become aroused or have an orgasm because it may trigger an asthma attack. As a result, they became dependent on an inhaler. If you want to use sexual healing for respiratory ailments, pay special attention to the breathing, relaxation, and arousal exercises and do them by yourself before you start working with your partner. Working alone first will help you learn to become aroused slowly and to breathe more deeply at the same time as you become aroused.

If during any exercise, your breathing becomes ragged, back off to an exercise you are comfortable with.

Skin Problems   These include conditions such as eczema and psoriasis. If you use a topical medication, apply it by rubbing it on in a sensate focus way, or have your partner do this. If your condition is contagious, your partner can use gloves. Your focus for this healing is to bring blood flow to the skin. All the arousal exercises will accomplish this, including those for arousal awareness, peaking, and plateauing. Any exercises with intercourse and other exercises that lead to orgasm will also get a healthful skin flush going.

Immune System Disorders These are conditions such as arthritis. If you have painful, swollen joints, you may not be able to caress yourself, so you may need your partner to do it. Find comfortable positions in which your weight is not on your joints; for example, use a side-to-side position for intercourse. Pay special attention to genital caresses. Your goal is to become as aroused as you can without making painful body movements. This will increase endorphin production and relieve some of your pain. You may also find it helpful for your partner to give mild sensate focus caresses on the affected joints.

Chronic Pain Chronic pain can occur anywhere, sexual healing is especially good for pain in the muscles of the back, neck, and shoulders. Relaxation, breathing, and sensate focus caresses on the affected area will help relax your body and alleviate pain. I recommend caressing for about fifteen to twenty minutes in a warm, comfortable room. Exercises that encourage prolonged arousal will also stimulate pain-killing endorphins.

Migraines Migraine is a specific severe form of headache caused by blood flow problems and muscle tension, usually triggered by stress. To treat migraines, the goal is to either increase blood flow to the brain or draw the flow away from it. Both approaches will work. If you are not in the middle of a migraine attack, usher more blood flow into your head area by doing a face caress. Pay special attention to the frontalis muscle between the eyebrows. If you are in the middle of a migraine attack, try a front caress and a genital caress to increase blood flow to your genital area. This will also increase endorphin production and relieve pain. Then, continue with relaxation exercises and eventually move to arousal awareness and peaking. In some rare cases migraines can occur after orgasm because of changes in the blood flow pattern. If this is a problem for you, you might prevent it by altering your arousal pattern to include slow, predictable stimulation, or by becoming multiply orgasmic and having a series of small orgasms instead of one big orgasm.

Gastrointestinal Problems   These include ulcers, colitis, and irritable bowel syndrome. These conditions are very common in men with premature ejaculation and men and women with inhibited orgasm. Again, sensate focus caresses will bring blood flow to the genitals from the periphery of the body. To bring about healing, try genital caresses, peaking, plateauing, and orgasm—any exercise or series of exercises that will relax your abdominal muscles and increase blood to flow to your pelvis.

Menstrual Problems   These include premenstrual syndrome, cramps, or irregular periods. Pelvic problems and PMS respond well to sexual healing, and these conditions are among the easiest problems to treat. Pelvic massage and orgasm are well-known and effective treatments for menstrual cramps. In addition, relief can be found with sensate focus caresses on the abdomen, genital caresses, peaking, and any sexual healing exercise up through orgasm.

Enlarged Prostate   Regular ejaculation can have a beneficial effect on benign prostate hypertrophy (BPH), commonly called enlarged prostate. But how often is regular, especially if you are an older man? You can usually tell by the color of your semen. Healthy semen is whitish, not yellowish. However, don't force yourself to ejaculate if you don't feel like it—you can use peaking and plateauing to feel better. Regular ejaculation will not prevent prostate cancer, because cancer usually has a genetic or toxic basis.

It is important for men to have a regular digital exam plus a PSA blood study. Some writers on tantra believe that a man should have orgasm but not ejaculate, that ejaculation depletes your "vital essence." All medical research I am familiar with, however, recommends regular ejaculation, especially for men over age fifty.

General Lack of Physical Conditioning You can actually use lovemaking to help yourself get into better overall shape. Making love is a great aerobic activity. Positions that require you to kneel, stand, squat, or put your legs back will all help develop your flexibility.

Sexual Healing of Stress Disorders

If you have medical conditions related to a stress disorder, all the exercises in this book will help your symptoms, especially the Belly Breathing and Deep Muscle Relaxation exercises in Chapter 6. However, be aware that if you want to get rid of those stress-related disorders for good, you will have to get rid of the stressor! This may mean changing your life in some fundamental way. Relaxation and breathing exercises will take care of the symptoms on a short-term basis, but you can't live with a severe stressor forever—sooner or later your medical problems will escalate.

Making love can act as a buffer against stress in general. A large part of the effect of stress has to do with how we interpret or experience it. You may ultimately find through sexual healing that the things that once stressed you out no longer have the power to do so.

Sexual Healing of Chronic Illnesses

Sick people need love too. In fact, they probably need it more than the rest of us, but for various reasons chronically ill people are less likely to make love. It is heartbreaking to visit a hospital and see chronically ill people shriveling up from lack of human contact because others are afraid to touch them. If you have a chronic illness, one that is not considered "curable," you may be looking for relief on a daily basis. Sexual healing for you focuses on how to cope and make love, rather than on how to heal the illness specifically. This is an area where healing comes from the power of your loving relationship.

Chronic illnesses such as lupus, Parkinson's, or MS present special healing circumstances. Although these illnesses often don't have sexual side effects, they may have psychological ones. This is because our society harbors an unhealthy attitude toward illness. We sometimes blame a person for the illness and hold it against him or her. We focus on the connection between appearance and sexuality. And we invest chronic illness with our fears: fear of disfigurement, fear that the illness is contagious, fear that an ill person will smell bad, or fear that making love will hurt the person who is ill. Touch becomes even more vital, because of the physical and psychological distance chronically ill people face.

I have had unique experiences with clients suffering from a variety of chronic illnesses. As a surrogate, I worked with people with cancer, heart disease, MS, Parkinson's . . . just about every condition you could name. Some people were affected sexually, others were not. Many simply had to make adjustments in the way they made love. My background in health psychology and my familiarity with all these issues put me in a unique position to work sexually with these clients. I understand the stigma that chronic illness can create, but I also understand that your skin and your brain are the true sex organs—intimacy and genital sexuality are not the same thing. Everyone appreciates touch, regardless of whether they are Quasimodo or a beauty queen. If you have a partner who has one of these conditions, the best thing you can do to heal your partner is embrace this attitude.

Healing Conditions
Caused by Physical Trauma

Many people with medical conditions resulting from physical trauma face physical or mobility challenges. Others may have disfigurements. These conditions can limit their physical sexual potential, from their ability to feel sensations to their ability to have intercourse. They also may limit the potential of finding a sexual partner through common channels.

If you or your partner have one of these conditions, which exercises will help you heal? Any and all of them. I encourage you to do all the exercises that you are able to do. If you have physical limitations, work around them. Be creative. The major adjustment to make is in your attitude, not in the extent of your physical exercises. While I am not naive enough to think that lovemaking will completely heal a chronic, degenerative disease, I have seen truly miraculous changes take place in relationships in which one partner had a condition resulting from trauma. I'd like to share with you others' experiences of this wonderful sexual healing in hopes they might help you.

I once treated a couple in which the husband had prostate cancer. He opted to have his prostate removed. As a result, he was incontinent for a few months. What adjustments did he and his wife make? They had to change a sheet once in a while—that's it. Eventually he had a penile implant put in, which required a bit more adjustment. This was where sensate focus was very important: it helped his wife get over the feeling that she was having sex with a machine rather than a person. His adjustment involved realizing that having an erection whenever you want to doesn't mean you feel like making love. What exercises did they find especially healing? The sensate focus caresses, such as the genital caress.

A colleague of mine treated a woman who developed breast cancer and had a mastectomy. Her cancer was very advanced with poor prognosis, and there was a strong chance that she wouldn't make it. Her husband spent time physically loving her with massage, caressing, peaking, and plateauing. Through work with the Body Image exercises (Chapter 6), she and her husband made such strides in healing their relationship that their lovemaking became better than ever. She survived. And when she was out of the woods, she opted not to have her breast reconstructed.

I knew a woman, *Alicia,* who was one week away from dying of an extremely rare form of lung cancer. I believe her husband, *Tom,* kept her alive through his sheer force of will. Somehow, even when things looked darkest, he managed to convey to her the expectation that she was going to make it. Even when Alicia gave up, Tom wouldn't let her go. He did this by keeping and sharing his sense of humor throughout her illness. When she was well enough to leave the hospital, she had a catheter inserted in her chest for medication. Alicia wanted to go swimming with her daughter, but her daughter was concerned how people would react to the tube. Tom said, "Just tell everyone you have an inflatable mom."

As a surrogate partner, I treated a client with early-stage multiple sclerosis. Before coming to therapy he had been very depressed and was drinking a lot. *Jerry* sought therapy because he wanted to know how much he could feel and how much he would be able to do if he actually were in a relationship. The sensate focus techniques helped him realize he *could* make love, and they gave him the confidence to seek out a loving partner. I credit sexual healing with his turnaround.

The tragic case of actor Christopher Reeve focused attention on the realities of life for people with spinal cord injuries. From what I understand, he and his wife have the potential for a sexual healing relationship. What can a person experience after a spinal cord injury? Some can have erections, which is what everybody focuses on; others cannot. People's range of feeling—and their awareness of arousal—vary. I worked with a client with quadriplegia, who had movement only in his face (fortunately, this included his tongue). We were creative and worked with touch that he could feel, such as massage. With position adjustments, he found he was able to kiss and have oral sex. Although his physical areas of sensation were limited, his sense of arousal and physiological response was acute. He described what he experienced as "brain orgasms."

Another client, *Marcus,* had cerebral palsy, which limited his voluntary movement to the use of one arm. His speech was slow, and he used a wheelchair. However, because the penis has no voluntary muscles, he discovered that his erections were unaffected, and so his sexual response was completely normal. Through sexual healing, Marcus realized his sexual potential and healed his sense of self. He left therapy feeling that there was another aspect of life that was still open to him.

If your partner has a chronic illness, you may need to make some adjustments, too. Ultimately, the lesson here is not to focus on what a person with a chronic illness or a disability can or cannot "do" but to share fully in healing touch and to honor each other's experiences.

Natural Healers

Throughout history, in many different cultures, there have been people revered as "natural healers." Their touch just seems to do wonders for people. Could you be one of these people? You will never know until you try. The following exercises are designed to draw out your natural healing ability. As you share in these exercises, remember to convey positive, healthful expectations to your partner and to visualize healing energy flowing from you into your partner.

♀ Exercise ♂
Caress without Touching

Begin by doing a slow, focused front caress with your partner. Then concentrate caresses on one area of the body that needs healing. After focusing your healing energies, raise your hand just off your partner's skin. This is similar to the palm energy exercise you learned in Chapter 3.

Let's say your partner has menstrual cramps, and you wish to help heal her. Caress her abdomen, then move your hand so it is not touching her skin but is so close that you can feel the energy flow between you. Alternate actually lightly touching and not touching so that you can barely tell if you are touching or not. You can use this caress on any part of the body.

♀ Exercise ♂
From the Heart

Caress your partner's body, giving time to the area that needs healing. With healing intention, place your other hand lightly over your partner's heart. Do a nontouching caress over your partner's heart as you caress the part of his or her body that needs healing. You may also want to try lightly placing your ear over your partner's heart during the caress.

If Intercourse Is Not in the Cards

If you are a person whose partner needs healing from trauma, you may need to explore and redefine your understanding of sex, sexiness, and sexual consummation. You may not be able to make love with your partner in a conventional way. But that's not the point: sexual relating is a unique, individual union between every couple. If intercourse is not an option for you, there will be ways of making love that are. You might consider joining a support group in which people who have made similar adjustments share their experiences. If you are a person who needs physical healing and you don't have a partner, I hope this book encourages you to seek healing help. I only wish there were more surrogate partners out there to help you. Perhaps this book can inspire the profession.

♀ Exercise ♂
Mutual Masturbation

Masturbation is one of the most personal, intimate things that we experience. Many of us feel it is so private that we are hesitant to share this experience with a partner. However, if illness prevents you from having intercourse or otherwise caressing each other, try sharing masturbation.

There are two ways to do this. One way is for both of you to masturbate at the same time. Lie together on the bed and stimulate yourself the way you would if you were alone. Pay attention to your own arousal and send that energy out to your partner. If you wish, look deeply at each other as you become more and more aroused.

Another way to do this is to take turns masturbating while the other watches. This is a very intimate act, to share your most private activity with another. Try not to be self-conscious about your partner watching you, but concentrate on sexual energy. Relax, close your eyes, and pleasure yourself the way you like to most.

Mutual masturbation will get sexual energy flowing between you two even if you can't caress or make love in more conventional ways. As a result, healing can still take place.

♀ Exercise ♂
Sharing Fantasies

Here is another exercise that you can do if illness or physical limitations prevent caressing. It is commonly used by people who have spinal cord injuries. If you can talk, you can share a fantasy.

Share a fantasy, caressing each other with words. As you talk, the person who is able to can caress the person who is ill, or can masturbate. Again, focus on the flow and exchange of sexual healing energy. As the song says, "Fantasy can set you free."

*Photograph by
Charlotte Morrison*

Chapter 10

Healing Men's
Sexual Problems

lthough the focus in *Sexual Healing* is on the healing power of sexuality and how sexual touch can heal emotions, physical problems, and relationships, I have included two extensive chapters on treating specific male and female sexual problems. Because they often go untreated and are stigmatized, I feel it is important to discuss these issues here.

Some experts believe that if you heal your emotions, work on your relationship, and love each other, then all sexual problems will work themselves out. I disagree. I've known couples who had a great marriage, wonderful children, career success, enough money, everything you could want—and their sex life was still lousy. Why? Because many sexual problems spring from a life of faulty learning, and people need specific exercises to unlearn them.

While I believe that it is possible to heal specific sexual problems without being in a loving relationship, I also believe that there is a better chance your sexual problems will be healed if you approach them in the context of an intimate, loving relationship. For example, overcoming premature ejaculation, a very common male sexual problem, is largely a matter of understanding and practicing the mechanics of the PC muscle and ejaculation. A man can learn the *mechanics* of ejaculation control by himself without having a relationship with a lover, but if that same man heals his sexual problems *with* his partner, he ultimately learns to how make love, not just how to have better ejaculations. He also has the opportunity to develop more control specifically during intercourse.

And, he is surrounded by his partner's loving acceptance of him. Regardless of whether you are in an intimate relationship or not, these exercises will help improve your sexual functioning—they are that powerful.

The most common sexual problems that men encounter are low sexual desire, rapid ejaculation, erection problems (impotence), and inhibited male orgasm and ejaculation, and these are discussed below.

Low Sexual Desire

What has happened to a man who once had a stable desire for sex but no longer feels this desire? In some cases, especially with older men, this lack of sex drive is caused by a deficiency of the hormone testosterone. If you or your partner is experiencing a complete lack of sex drive, it is best to have a physician check your testosterone levels. It is rare for men to have clinically significant low testosterone levels. If you check out with normal levels, you might try boosting your levels by regular genital stimulation and activity.

If testosterone deficiency is not the cause, examine the influences in your life. There can be nonbiological, nonphysical causes for lack of desire. I tend to think of them in three categories, ranging from least to most serious. First, things like temporary stress, lack of sexual knowledge or experience, and lack of stimulating activities can put a damper on sexual inspiration. These influences are relatively easy to remedy: if you are stressed out, increasing relaxation (your ability to relax *and* your opportunities to relax) is key. A day off or a weekend away will give your desire a chance to grow. Exploring sexually informative materials such as books, videos, or audiotapes can also go a long way toward sparking desire.

The next level of causes is mild depression and anxiety. Again, these are fairly straightforward to alleviate with relaxation exercises and other treatments. Temporary "fixes" for anxiety and depression include almost any change in routine. Laughter is a simple and effective boost: go out and do something fun; rent funny movies; reach out to entertaining friends.

If your low sexual desire is because of the first two types of causes mentioned, the exercises in *Sexual Healing* will work wonders for you, especially the front, back, and genital caresses in Chapter 5.

A more serious cause of low sexual desire is the repression or denial of some traumatic event in the past. If you suspect this is the case for you, seek the help of a qualified therapist. While other tactics may provide band-aid approaches that temporarily stimulate your desire, the only permanent solution is to get at the root of the issue and work through the effects of the trauma.

Ejaculation Control

Premature ejaculation, sometimes called rapid ejaculation, is not defined by how long you last (whether in seconds or minutes), how many strokes you can take before ejaculation, or whether your partner has an orgasm. Rather, premature ejaculation occurs when you ejaculate before you wish, when you don't feel in control of your ejaculation.

Some experts think it should not matter how long a man's erection lasts. They believe how long a man is able to have inter-course before he ejaculates is not important: if he ejaculates before he wants to, he can simply continue to have intercourse with a flaccid penis. After spending many years treating men with premature ejacu-lation, I get upset when I read these ideas. I have seen too many men psychologically devastated by this problem. They find this condition intolerable because they want to last longer when making love—both to more fully please their partner and to spend a longer time enjoying lovemaking without worry and without pressure. In addition, I find that the length of time a man lasts during love-making can affect his opportunity to experience the healing touch of his partner. Premature ejaculation can be a serious sexual problem if it detracts from the ability to heal and be healed sexually.

You don't have to be a marathon man, but you should have enough ejaculation control that you can control it about 75 percent of the time. It is normal to ejaculate before you want to some of the time, especially if you are young, if you don't have sex regularly, or if you are with a new partner. This is not a cause for alarm and it is nothing to be ashamed of. If you have ever had control, you have the ability to have it again, and for life. The exercises in this chapter are for men who have not learned ejaculation control or who, for a situational reason (stress, anxiety), do not have it now.

It is important to remember, too, that the quality of making love is not dependent on the quantity, the amount of activity. I believe in ejaculation control for life rather than making love for a certain length of time. Sometimes you and your lover may want to spend long periods of time in the types of healing intercourse that I described in Chapter 8. At other times you may just want a quickie. Both celebrate your intimacy, so you should have the pleasure of these options—but with premature ejaculation you don't.

Premature ejaculation is actually an easy problem to deal with, especially when your partner is willing to help you. You will need to make a time commitment of about three hours a week to tap into the sexual power that the exercises in this chapter develop. By the end of around six weeks your control should be much more satisfactory. If you are trying to cure any of the other sexual problems described in this chapter or the next, I recommend that you be very diligent about setting aside a specific time each week to work with them, particularly if you and your partner lead busy lives. This program is one of learning and behavior change, and a predictable schedule is vital in this effort.

If you are working through this book to heal your relationship in general, you may enjoy the benefits of these exercises, so I encourage you to try them whenever you feel like it.

What Causes Premature Ejaculation?

Premature ejaculation occurs when your PC muscle spasms out of control and causes you to ejaculate. This response is caused by anxiety, both short-term and long-term. Short-term anxiety causes your body to tense up, including your PC muscle. Long-term anxiety can build if you are conscious about a tendency to ejaculate quickly, and when faced with temporary stress or tension (such as being with a new partner), will make the situation worse.

Any program to teach you ejaculation control will encourage three things: control of your PC muscle, the ability to truly relax, and intense awareness of your sensations. This is why the conventional wisdom—thinking about something else during intercourse to make it last longer—doesn't work. You can only control your arousal and ejaculation if you are paying attention to your body, not ignoring it.

♀ A Program ♂
to Treat Premature Ejaculation

If you would like to gain control of your ejaculation for life, try the following program.

- Do the PC muscle exercises described in Chapter 4 every day.

- Do the belly breathing described in Chapter 6 every day as well.

- Once you are in touch with your body's responses and abilities, move on to the solo sensate focus caress and the genital caress described in Chapter 2.

- Next, practice the arousal awareness, peaking, and plateauing exercises from Chapter 6 by yourself. Try these one to three times a week, depending on how much free time you have.

When you feel more in control and aware of your sexual energy, you can begin working with your partner. Do one or two partner exercises a week—no more, no less. You want to build sexual healing energy and intimacy as well as ejaculation control.

- First, enjoy the intimacy of the bonding exercises and the face, front, back, and genital caresses with your partner (Chapters 3 and 5).

- Then try the exercises below, Peaking with a PC Squeeze and First Intercourse for Premature Ejaculation.

- After those exercises you can move on to the peaking and plateauing exercises in Chapter 7. Repeat these exercises until you can last 20 minutes.

- Try side-to-side intercourse until you can last 20 minutes.

- When your ejaculation control has improved and you feel secure with it at that point, try the advanced sexual healing intercourse exercises in Chapter 8. Can you last 20 minutes with each of them?

What happens if you have completed the peaking and plateauing exercises in Chapter 7 but still don't feel you have the control you desire? You may need to adjust the exercises, and your expectations during them, slightly. For example, during exercises such as the genital caress, peaking, and plateauing, don't worry about ejaculating and don't hold back. If you ejaculate during one of the exercises before you want to, just enjoy it. I mean it: really look forward to ejaculation whenever it comes, and start *enjoying* your climax instead of apologizing for it.

You may also find that during peaking and plateauing, your partner can adjust her caresses to allow you more time between peaks. You might try some of the exercises more than once, until you have control with manual and oral peaking for about fifteen to twenty minutes. At that point, keep working with the following exercises, which specifically address ejaculation control.

♀ Exercise ♂
Peaking with a PC Squeeze

Learning to use your PC muscle to put the brakes on your arousal is a little tricky. Normally, if you reach a certain level of arousal and then quickly squeeze the PC muscle once or twice, your arousal will go down a level. The reason this takes a little time to learn is that there are several different ways to squeeze. You may have to experiment a little bit to see which one works for you. Work with this on your own first before you try it with your partner.

There are three basic types of PC muscle squeezes: one long hard squeeze, two medium squeezes, or several quick squeezes in a row, similar to the PC muscle spasms during ejaculation. (You may be wondering who took the time to figure this out . . . well, we used to have debates about it at work.)

Before You Begin   Experiment with a genital caress by yourself and do some peaks. During the peaks, try different PC squeezes. You want to find the smallest PC squeeze that will take your arousal down a level without affecting your erection. If you squeeze your PC muscle too much before you have a full erection, you may temporarily lose your erection. Don't worry, however, it will come back in a few minutes.

The Exercise   Find the best way to squeeze your PC muscle by calling on your arousal awareness during a peaking exercise. At each peak, recognize your arousal level and squeeze your PC muscle. Let your arousal peak at levels six, seven, eight, and nine. Then let go in an orgasm without trying to hold back. Repeat this exercise two or three times on different days, then try it with your partner.

With Your Partner   With your partner, give front and genital caresses to inspire your arousal. As you begin to peak, tell your partner your level and squeeze your PC muscle in your preferred way. Let your partner caress you through arousal peaks. At each peak after you squeeze, breathe and relax your muscles. Continue peaking and see if you can use your PC to lower your arousal even at level nine. Then release yourself to have an orgasm and ejaculate if you wish.

Once you have done this exercise you are ready for intercourse. This first time you make love, do it in a very specific way. After that, indulge in intercourse peaking and plateauing as described in Chapter 8.

♀ Exercise ♂
First Intercourse
for Premature Ejaculation

Before You Begin   Peak with hand and oral stimulation to levels four, five, and six. Then lie on your side facing your partner, as she lies on her back. Interweave your legs so that your genitals are up against each other. This is a comfortable side-to-side position, in which neither person is on top.

The Exercise   Stroke a lot of lubrication on your penis and around your partner's vagina. Now slowly insert your penis, whether it is flaccid, erect, or somewhere in between. Relax all your muscles, breathe, and note your arousal level. If it is a six or under, begin slow pelvic rolls and thrusts, and start peaking. Peak at levels five, six, seven and eight, stopping in between for as long as you need. See if you can do several peaks for about fifteen minutes, then ejaculate if you desire.

If your arousal level is higher than six when you first insert your penis, withdraw and allow your arousal to go down, then re-enter even if you are flaccid. If all you are able to do this first time is lie inside your partner without moving, that's fine—it is progress. Enjoy the sexual intimacy it brings. You should keep repeating the exercise until you can recognize your arousal levels and move inside your partner. Breathe, relax, focus. You will do fine.

After you can do the side-to-side position for fifteen minutes, try the peaking exercise in different positions as described in Chapter 8. The only difference between you and someone who is not concerned with ejaculation is you may have to move a little slower, repeat exercises, or use your PC muscle at some of your peaks.

If Your Partner Has Premature Ejaculation

If your partner has premature ejaculation, you may feel very frustrated. This is a perfect opportunity for you to be a sexual healer for your partner and yourself. You should try some of the sexual healing exercises alone to prepare yourself for healing your partner. By doing so, you will become familiar with what your partner is learning, and with terms like peaking and plateauing. You will also learn about your own arousal and can become more orgasmic, so that you won't need your partner to last a certain amount of time.

Also, explore your attitude and expectation, for example the sexual energy you have been expressing to your partner. In the past you may have felt he ejaculates quickly because he is selfish, and doesn't care if you are satisfied. To heal some of these attitudes, try the self-touch exercises in Chapter 2 and the belly breathing and self-arousal exercises in Chapter 6. You and your partner can also share in the bonding exercises in Chapter 3.

When the time comes to work with your partner, your attitude will be very important. Caress him slowly, with healing care, and don't pressure him. If he does ejaculate before he wants to in any exercise, continue with the exercise or start again. As you peak and plateau together you will learn his arousal patterns, so you will know when to stop and start stimulation. Don't forget to ask your partner to indulge in peaking or plateauing exercises with you, so that he too can get to know your arousal patterns more deeply. Ultimately, you two will discovermore intimate experiences of each other's arousal, stronger sexual harmony, and more mutual satisfaction.

When to Get Professional Help

If your premature ejaculation problem is severe, you may need professional help—not because you can't do it yourself, but because you may need someone to motivate you and guide you through the exercises. Remember that premature ejaculation is 100 percent treatable, and if you find you can't seem to make the time to exercise, see a therapist who specializes in treating sexual problems. You may find that you are actually doing something to prevent yourself from succeeding, such as tensing the pelvic muscles or unconsciously sabotaging your success by making appointments with your partner and then not keeping them.

Prozac is currently under investigation as a treatment for premature ejaculation. Some men have had success with it; on average it increases time in intercourse from about one minute to three to four minutes. Prozac does not inhibit ejaculation as such, but it reduces anxiety, which allows men to last longer.

Satisfying Erections

This is a big area of concern for men and an area in which healing is really needed. I often think that if you gave men a choice between having a full range of sexual feelings, arousal, and desire, or having a rock-hard erection whenever they wanted it but no feeling, the majority would choose the erection. This attitude is sad, because one result is that a lot of men who don't really need penile implants get them anyway. Also, it prompts men to put pressure on themselves and on their partners when they could be making love instead. Sure, women get concerned when their partner's functioning is not up to par. But most women want to make love with a partner, not a penis.

Unfortunately, the medical community contributes to this unhealthy attitude. The biggest breakthroughs in treating sexual problems in the past few years have been medical, including penile implants, vacuum pumps to create erections, and penile injections. I believe the medical community does men a disservice by convincing them that most erection problems are physical. This tendency to view our bodies as machines that need fixing ultimately stands in the way of sexual healing and lovemaking, because we are our minds *and* bodies, and we just don't work that way.

What Is a "Normal" Erection?

Your erection reflects the state of your physical health and your psychological health. Erection problems have various causes, including medical conditions, stress, and relationship problems. While most men consider erections an all-or-nothing phenomenon (either you have one or you don't), this is not true. A man can have a partial erection and still make love. A man can have a completely flaccid penis and still make love. No matter the hardness of his erection, he can feel every level of arousal through orgasm.

For the purpose of understanding more about erections, think of them on a scale of one to ten. This is not the same as the arousal scale you learned in Chapter 6. Here we are concerned with how hard your erection is, not what you are feeling. On the erection scale, level one is no erection—a completely flaccid penis. Levels two through four are what is called filling: blood begins to flow into the penis and it becomes warmer and thicker. Anything beyond level five is rigidity—that "spring back" quality. A level ten is an extremely hard erection, one that is almost painful.

Based on this scale, are you really sure you have erection problems? If you regularly have a level seven or level eight erection and are able to make love and not worry about your erection, you don't have a problem. If you are unable to have an erection once in a while, after drinking too much, for example, but have an erection most times that you desire one, again, this is normal. It is also normal for your erection level to go up and down during a session of lovemaking. However, if you are not able to have an erection at all, or you regularly lose it before penetration, read on.

Could Your Erection Problem Be Physical?

If you have decided you have an erection problem and you wish to heal it, the first thing to recognize is that your erection problem might be physical. Before consulting a physician and getting a lot of expensive medical tests, ask yourself the following questions:

- Do I have an erection at night or when I wake up in the morning?

- Do I have morning or nighttime erections, but have trouble when I'm with my partner?

- Do I have erections when masturbating but not when I'm with my partner?

A healthy man has several erections during the night, and erections with masturbation. If you answered yes to any of these questions, your difficulty may have a psychological root and you will benefit from the exercises in this chapter.

If you never have morning or night erections and haven't for several years, try the exercises anyway. There is the chance you have a physical problem, but the exercises won't hurt you, and I've seen them work wonders for men with organic impotence because of the powerful effect the mind has on the body. If you go through this program and experience no improvement, I recommend you see an urologist who specializes in erection problems. If you do not get erections when you masturbate (when psychological pressure is off), you might very well have a medical problem, and seeking medical advice is in order.

More Fulfilling Erections

There are specific points of mind-body connection that may be getting in the way of satisfying erections.

Attitude   The first place to start is with your attitude and sexual awareness. Never pressure yourself to have an erection during any exercise. You can do every exercise in this book, up to and including intercourse, without an erection. While working through the exercises in this book, pay more attention to your arousal levels than you do to your erection. You will find that erections aren't the center of your sexual energy; they are part of it, an expression.

Health Habits   After examining your attitude, take a look at your health habits. Are you overweight? Do you smoke, drink alcohol, or use illegal drugs? As I mentioned in Chapter 4, all of these can cause severe erection problems. Quitting these practices will make dramatic changes in your erections and your sexual fulfillment, your ability to savor sensations, and ultimately, your self-esteem.

Medical Conditions Do you have any chronic medical conditions that might be affecting your erections? Diabetes, prostate problems, and circulation problems are among the medical conditions that can interfere with erections. In addition, many prescription medications, such as those given for high blood pressure and ulcers, can affect erections.

Emotions Lastly, look at your emotional landscape. Are you depressed, anxious, or stressed out? Are you alienated from or unhappy with your partner? Is your relationship a mess? No wonder you can't get an erection!

Pelvic Steal In addition to all of the physical and emotional problems that can affect your erections, it is also possible that you may be doing something during lovemaking that prevents your erection. Unconsciously or consciously squeezing your PC muscle during arousal can actually prevent erection. As you become aroused, you may also unconsciously tighten the muscles in your legs, abdomen, or buttocks. Some men do this because they think it helps them get an erection. In fact, it does the opposite, because the blood that could be available for your erection is diverted to the muscles that are tightening up. This situation is called pelvic-steal syndrome: the blood that could be used for your erection is literally being stolen by the long muscles in your body.

Spectatoring Finally, are you spectatoring? This is a phrase coined by Masters and Johnson that refers to watching and worrying about whether you are getting an erection. A watched pot never boils . . . and a watched penis never hardens.

♀ A Program ♂
for Erection Problems

If you have erection problems and you would like to heal them using this program, there is one exercise you should do every day and that is the Daily Genital Massage (see below).

In addition to this massage, you should work through a series of exercises:

- Begin with the self-touch exercises from Chapter 2.

- Invite your partner to do the bonding exercises from Chapter 3.

- Develop your PC muscle and spend time learning to relax your other muscles with exercises from Chapter 4.

- Then move on to the Belly Breathing, Peaking, and Plateauing exercises from Chapter 6.

- When you feel your sexual healing energy is strong, try the beginning sexual healer caresses in Chapter 5.

During all these exercises, don't pressure yourself to have an erection. Don't even pay attention to whether you have one or not. Your partner can always let you know whether you had one after an exercise. If have an erection and it goes down, don't panic. Slow down, relax, and refocus. These exercises will help you a lot and they may be all you need.

If you have reliable, satisfying erections during these exercises, proceed to the advanced sexual healer and intercourse described in Chapters 7 and 8. If you are still having erection problems, try the following very specific exercises before you proceed to intercourse.

♀ Exercise ♂
Daily Genital Massage

Every day, for ten minutes, gently massage your penis, especially around the base. This is a way to get more blood flowing to the genital area. Put simply, this will help "prime the pump."

Don't massage to create an erection. Massage to become aware of your penis and its sensations. This makes or reinforces your mind-body connection, which is crucial to experiencing deep arousal. Gentle massage will help develop your sensate focus awareness, similar to the earlier self-touch exercises in this book.

Do this massage whether you have an erection or not. I promise you will see the results in future exercises.

♀ Exercise ♂
Erection Awareness

Believe it or not, some men are so out of touch with their own body that they do not know whether they have an erection or not. Basic sensate focus exercises such as the face, back, front, and genital caress have helped you learn to experience sensations. If you do not have erection awareness, you may experience pleasant feelings but not be aware that your penis is hard enough for intercourse. I've worked with many clients who have this problem. It was common to have a session in which I would give a genital caress for twenty minutes or so and the client would have an erection almost the entire time without realizing it. Eventually the erection would go away simply because a lot of time had elapsed, and the client would think that in fact he had not had an erection at all.

Another cause for lack of erection awareness is that many men specifically learn to ignore their erections because they think it is the best way to get an erection. Actually this is partially on the right track. You need to stop *worrying about* your genitals and start *feeling* them. You want to concentrate on your genital sensations, not ignore them.

Before You Begin To practice erection awareness with a partner, think of the hardness of your erection on the one-to-ten scale I mentioned earlier in this chapter. Remember that level one is a completely flaccid penis, level five is the beginning of rigidity (that spring back quality), and level ten is an extremely hard, almost painful erection. If you have morning erections or erections when you masturbate, practice describing them with this scale.

The Exercise For this first erection awareness exercise, lie on your back. Your partner will begin a slow, focused front caress and genital caress for about twenty minutes. At various points she will ask you how strong you think your erection is. If her estimate differs significantly from yours, she will ask you to open your eyes and look at your penis.

If you describe your erection as a two (beginning filling) when in fact it is a five (beginning rigidity, borderline hard) you need to believe this. After you have seen your erection, close your eyes again and concentrate on the feelings in your penis as your partner caresses you. This will help you learn to recognize the feelings of erection without having to look.

Remember to keep your PC muscle relaxed. Keep your leg muscles relaxed, and breathe and focus. Your partner will ask you your erection level several more times. If you begin to feel pressured to have an erection, back up to an earlier level of filling. There may not be that much variation in erections the first time you do the exercise. If you only go to level two or three, you have still made progress. Repeat the exercise as many times as you need to until you can reliably recognize some degree of rigidity.

Without a Partner It is wonderful to have a partner to help you with this awareness, but you can easily adapt this exercise to do by yourself. Simply do a genital caress, estimate your hardness, and close and open your eyes to check your sensations with your perception.

The physiology of having and maintaining an erection is complex and beyond the scope of this book. In fact, we could write a whole book just about erections. Instead, let's talk about it in simple terms. Think about your partner giving you a genital caress or oral sex. When you are breathing deeply and evenly and not holding your breath, your partner will be able to feel and even see blood flow into your penis. If you hold your breath, she will be able to feel blood flow back out. If you keep your abdomen, thigh, and buttocks muscles completely relaxed, blood will flow in. The instant you tighten up, blood will flow back out. When you keep your PC muscle relaxed, blood flows in. When you either consciously or unconsciously squeeze your PC muscle, blood flows back out again. This simple in-and-out process, which your partner can easily observe, is the basis of the next erection exercise.

What goes up must come down. We all accept this law of gravity in the abstract. However, when it comes to erections, many men believe—or hope—that what goes up will stay up forever! It is perfectly normal for erections to get harder and softer several times during the course of a sexual encounter. When men feel their erection start to get soft, whether it is during intercourse or before, they often panic and start frenzied activities to try to regain the erection or to use it before they lose it. Working at it or trying to keep it hard is the worst thing you can do, as it virtually guarantees that you will lose the erection.

If you are one of those men who panics when an erection starts to go down, you need to learn a new response to this situation. Your previous response may have been, "What if she thinks there's something wrong with me?" or "Oh no! I'm losing it. I need to hurry up and do something before it goes down completely." Surprisingly, what you really need to do is just the opposite.

You have learned to believe that once you lose an erection, it will never come back. It is obvious how you learned this: in previous situations when you lost an erection, you worried about it, and this guaranteed that it never came back.

Whenever you get that panicked feeling because you are losing an erection, you need to use it as a signal to tell yourself the opposite: "I'm losing it! I need to relax and enjoy the sensations in my penis. I need to make sure that I don't try to work at anything sexual when I am feeling anxious. I need to take a deep breath, relax my leg muscles, and focus on how my partner is touching me." Your erection will come back.

♀ Exercise ♂
Getting and Losing Erections

This getting-and-losing exercise will help you develop a new, effective response for times when you feel your erection go down. What goes up must come down, but that's not such a bad thing.

The Exercise   To begin the exercise, lie on your back with your eyes closed. Your partner will begin a pressure-free front caress and a manual and oral genital caress. Whenever you get a noticeable erection (even if it is only filling at levels two, three, and four), your partner will stop the stimulation and allow your erection to go all the way back down. Then she will start caressing again. If you get another erection, she will stop. Each time during the caress she will let the erection get a little harder before she stops. The two of you should repeat this a number of times during a twenty-minute period.

The first time you do this exercise, it may be frustrating. In fact, you may not have an erection at all, because you are worrying about it. If you do have an erection, you may be tempted to fall back on old habits of flexing your PC muscle, tensing your thighs, thrusting your pelvis, or holding your breath when you feel yourself losing the erection. Your partner can give you feedback on whether you are doing these things. She can help you monitor this so you become aware of the simple relationships: relaxation means blood flows in, tension means blood flows out.

When doing this exercise you may find that you are frustrated the first few times your partner stops her strokes. You may experience a little reverse psychology, thinking to yourself, "I'll show her! This time I'll get the erection and I won't lose it even though she stops stroking me." But you will—since this is the effect psychological pressure has.

Again, it is wonderful to be able to do this exercise with a partner, but it is also very effective by yourself.

♀ Exercise ♂
Flaccid Insertion

You may have been having partial erections but avoided having intercourse with them because you thought they weren't hard enough. If you tend to put a lot of pressure on yourself to have an erection, this exercise will show you the pleasures of intercourse without an erection. This technique is also wonderful if you have erection problems because of medical causes and you and your partner desire the healing intimacy of intercourse.

The Exercise   Lie on your side facing your partner, as she lies on her back with one leg on top of yours and the other in between. You will be at right angles to each other, with your genitals right up against each other.

Both of you should breathe and relax. Your partner then caresses your genitals and her own with lubricant. If you become partially erect during this, it is fine.

Regardless of your level of erection, your partner gently folds or "stuffs" your penis into her vagina. Your partner can open her vagina with her fingers, and sometimes it is helpful to slide a flaccid penis into the vagina using one or two fingers as a splint. Rather than inserting the head of the penis first, she can also place the penis along the labia with the base at the vaginal opening. Then she can gently push the base of the penis into the vagina. The tip will naturally follow. Another way to insert a flaccid penis is to hold it tightly around the base between two of your fingers and push it into the vagina with your other hand.

Your partner should then squeeze her PC muscle to make sure your penis is inside.

The purpose of this exercise is not to become aroused, but to experience being inside your partner with no pressure to have an erection or perform sexually. Once you are inside your partner, it may be tempting to move or thrust. The first time you do this exercise, try to remain as still as possible. Breathe and relax your legs. At most, squeeze your PC muscle once in a while to make sure you are still inserted. Focus on non-pressured physical union with your lover.

Repeat this exercise, each time adding a little more movement. Focus on the point of connection with your partner: her warmth, wetness, and the sexual energy of her vagina. Eventually, allow yourself to peak up to different levels of arousal (not erection). If you focus on what you are feeling and how aroused you are, you are more likely to get and maintain an erection.

You may also wish to try the exercise Peaking with Your Partner, described in Chapter 7. It is great for erections and rapid ejaculation. With it, you will find that your erection level follows your arousal level.

♀ Exercise ♂
Oral Sex with the Man on Top

Do you have erections reliably but find it difficult to get one when you are lying on your back? If so, experiment with oral-genital caresses in a different position. Instead of having oral sex while you lie on your back, kneel down and let your partner lie perpendicular to you on her side. A pillow or two may make her more comfortable. She can then caress your penis and do pressure-free, sensuous oral sex. It is a little more difficult to keep your legs relaxed when you are kneeling but a lot of men find that gravity gives them a little boost of blood flow.

If Your Partner Has Erection Problems

If your partner has erection problems, it is easy to blame yourself, or think he doesn't find you attractive. Though you may have been worried for some time, however, this is a good time for you to use your sexual healing powers. Never pressure your partner to have an erection, and don't express disappointment if he doesn't have one during an exercise. Relax, let go of your expectations, and focus on your current points of connection. When you do a sensate focus exercise with your partner, concentrate on the pleasures of touching him for yourself, not on using a touch that will give him an erection. Remember the power of a healing attitude. Stay close through the exercises—embrace him with your body and your sexual loving.

When to Get Professional Help

If you have done the exercises in this book and don't experience an improvement in your erections, you may have a medical problem. In that case, I recommend consulting an urologist who specializes in treating erection problems.

Inhibited Ejaculation and Orgasm

This problem was once called "ejaculatory incompetence" or "retarded ejaculation." This was quite confusing because orgasm and ejaculation are not the same thing. Orgasm is a delicious, full-body experience: it makes your heart pound, speeds up breathing, sends spasms through the long muscles in your arms and legs, and ends with an intense feeling of release. The energy built up in your body heightens to a peak and is released rapidly. Some people describe feeling an altered state of consciousness during orgasm. Ejaculation, on the other hand, is a physiological act: the release of semen, propelled by PC muscle spasms. A man can have an orgasm without ejaculating. He can also have an ejaculation without orgasm, without even feeling good. This happens to many men with rapid ejaculation. Not surprisingly, I have known many men who, once they learned to ejaculate, said "Is that all there is? That's what it's all about?" Most men feel that being able to have full orgasms is more satisfying and important than ejaculating.

Men's ejaculatory and orgasmic response are more complex than we once believed. For example, we now know that men can enjoy multiple orgasms the same way women can. (If you would like to learn this skill, see the exercises in Chapter 12 and read my recent book, *How to Make Love All Night.*)

Most men who experience inhibited ejaculation complain that they don't have an orgasm *or* ejaculate. They usually find this to be a problem only during intercourse. As far as causes are concerned, the thinking on this has changed recently. Sex therapists used to believe that inhibited ejaculation was caused by deep-seated psychological problems such as fear of intimacy or anger at women. We now know that it is more likely to do with learning, early sexual experience, and masturbation habits.

Typically, a man with inhibited ejaculation has overdeveloped his PC muscle, and he squeezes it very hard right before ejaculation. His instinct is that this will help him ejaculate, but, as you know, it does the opposite—it *prevents* ejaculation.

♀ A Program ♂ for Releasing Ejaculation and Orgasm

If you have difficulty ejaculating with intercourse, try the following program of exercises:

- Begin with the self-touch exercises in Chapter 2 and concentrate on keeping your PC muscle relaxed.

- Use the sexual fitness exercises in Chapter 4 to pay special attention to the phase of the PC muscle exercise in which you consciously relax the muscle in between squeezes, and the effects of PC squeezes on your erections and arousal.

- Invite your partner to explore the bonding exercises in Chapter 3, then do the beginning partner exercises in Chapter 5.

- By yourself, get comfortable with the arousal awareness, peaking, and plateauing exercises in Chapter 6—these are crucial for you. As you peak and plateau, keep your PC muscle as relaxed as you can.

- Conclude with the partner sexual healing exercises in Chapter 7 and the intercourse exercises in Chapter 8.

Because of the early exercises and the PC muscle relaxation, you will probably become more aroused during intercourse. If you are still unable to ejaculate with intercourse, start by limiting your time during intercourse. Don't keep going just because you think that the longer you spend, the more likely you are to ejaculate. It's not true. Peak during intercourse for twenty minutes at the most, then stop whether you have ejaculated or not. Back up and try the following exercises.

♀ Exercise ♂
Softening Your Stroke

If you are having difficulty ejaculating with intercourse, here is a special set of exercises to help sensitize your penis. They will help you become more aware of the delicate sensations of being inside your lover's vagina.

One of the most common causes of difficulty with ejaculation is a man's masturbation style. His stroke is either too fast or applies too much pressure, which desensitizes his penis. If you masturbate frequently (once a day or more), temporarily cut back in order to give yourself a little bit of an edge when you have intercourse. You can also try limiting your masturbation time. If you regularly spend half an hour or more for masturbation, try cutting it down to ten or fifteen minutes to retrain yourself to ejaculate more quickly. You may find, during this process, that different strokes can bring you to climax. Changing your stroke is the most important thing you can do.

The Exercise   Do a genital caress on yourself. Close your eyes and concentrate on the sensations of your touch. As you caress your genitals, slow down your stroke so that it is half as fast as when you began. Enjoy the sensations of this new stroke. What changes do you feel in your penis, your fingers?

Now slow down a second time, until your fingers and palm are barely moving over your penis. Continue this caress for fifteen minutes whether you ejaculate or not.

Use this exercise on a regular basis to decrease your masturbation frequency, time, and the roughness of your stroke. To help slow yourself down, you can try using your left hand if your are right-handed (or vice versa), or using an open palm or fingertips alone instead of using a closed fist.

♀ Exercise ♂
Alternating Peaks

This exercise is especially enjoyable because it encourages you to savor the unique touches of both oral stimulation and intercourse.

The Exercise   With your partner, begin a peaking exercise in which she does a genital caress with you up through level five. Focus on the sensations and texture of her touch. Then begin intercourse and peak up to level six. Again, really feel the sensations of your mutual touch.

Next, have your partner give an oral genital caress until you peak to the next level. Let yourself experience the different touches of her tongue and lips. Return to having intercourse until you reach the next peak.

Continue alternating oral caress peaks with intercourse peaks. Repeat the exercise until you are able to ejaculate with an intercourse peak.

As a variation on this exercise, you might also wish to alternate with peaks in which you stimulate yourself.

♀ Exercise ♂
Approaching Intercourse

This is another approach to inhibited ejaculation that I have seen work with many men. Do a peaking exercise with your partner in which you peak yourself up to level nine with your hand. When you feel on the verge of "the point of no return," insert your penis into your partner's vagina.

Repeat this exercise, enjoying the feel of ejaculation alongside that of your partner's vagina. Try entering just before "the point," until you can enter her at level eight or nine and ejaculate.

If Your Partner Has Inhibited Orgasm and Ejaculation

If your partner has inhibited ejaculation, you may not be frustrated but you may be sore. If you wish to help your partner heal this problem, the two best things you can do are help limit the time you spend having intercourse, and be patient. I've seen some success stories that took six months to a year to achieve.

When to Get Professional Help

If you have inhibited ejaculation that does not respond to these exercises, you may want to see a physician. There are several medical conditions that can cause inhibited ejaculation, including diabetes and multiple sclerosis. Some medications, such as monoamine oxidase inhibitors for depression, can also suppress ejaculation. If you are an older man, prostate problems can sometimes make both ejaculation and urination difficult.

Photograph by
Ralph Steinmeier

Chapter 11

Healing Women's Sexual Problems

he most common sexual problems women experience are lack of desire, difficulties with arousal and orgasm, and pain with intercourse. This chapter offers practical exercises to help you become aroused, have fulfilling orgasms, and triumph over sexual pain. By understanding your body better, you can strengthen the power of your mind-body connection.

Women's Sex Drive and Sexual Desire

Over the years, I've learned a lot about women's sex drive, and I *don't* believe that sex drive and sexual desire are the same thing. But both contribute to a woman's desire for intercourse and sexual intimacy.

Women's *sex drive* is fired by the hormone testosterone, the same hormone responsible for men's sex drive. (Contrary to most people's impressions, women produce testosterone too, but in much smaller amounts than men.) *Sexual desire,* on the other hand, is a complex interaction in which our mood, self-consciousness, intimate relationship, and the external circumstances affect our sexual interest and arousal.

Let's talk about sex drive first, since it is more straightforward. Our sex drive is dynamic, evolving with the hormonal changes in our life. These hormonal changes in turn are triggered by life changes. Pregnancy, childbirth, menopause, and surgery alter levels of hormones, particularly testosterone, thus increasing or decreasing sex drive. Birth control pills, because they synthetically regulate hormone levels, can also affect sexual urges. A good guide to the changes and cycles of desire in women is *Women, Sex and Desire,* by Elizabeth Davis.

If your sex drive has been strong in the past, it would be unusual for you to experience no desire to make love for a long time. If you are concerned that you have lost your sex drive (you never want to make love) and your surrounding conditions have not changed (you remain in love with your partner, are not unduly stressed, are not on the Pill or other hormonal medications), there may be a biological cause for this. I recommend you consult a endocrinologist, who can check your hormonal levels.

Desire, on the other hand, is nourished by our mindset. So stress, lack of sexual confidence or experience, and mild depression can all have negative effects. Low sexual desire is extremely common—in fact, in the 1980s so many people felt their desire succumb to stress and overwork that it came to be known as the "yuppie disease." Luckily it is very easily remedied. If you feel this is what is affecting you, the exercises in this book can help you relax, get comfortable with your sexual potential, and stir up your sexual desire.

A less common and more serious cause of low sexual desire is the repercussion of a traumatic event, particularly if it was of a sexual nature. We often cope with trauma, whether recent or past, by deflecting the experience within ourselves. If this is what you encounter, I urge you to seek professional help and give yourself permission to be sexually healed. Putting this trauma behind you will free you to embrace the full spectrum of your sexuality.

♀ A Program ♂
for Deepening Desire

In my experience, women's sexual desire is an intricate interplay of factors. It has as much—if not more—to do with love, acceptance, permission, body image, setting, and the attractiveness of their partner as it does with hormones or stress levels. We have all been in a situation where we didn't want to make love because we felt unattractive, we were stressed out, our partner wasn't communicating feelings, the laundry wasn't done, or we were worried about the kids or what we had to do the next day.

What is the solution? If you have certain conditions that need to be met before you make love, do your best to create those conditions—up to a point. Nothing can ever be perfect, but if you like to make love in a beautiful setting with flowers, scents, music, linens, then create that setting, even if only for one night! If you need to feel beautiful before you make love, set aside a special time to take a bath, give yourself a manicure and pedicure, do your hair, or put on a sexy outfit. All of these can boost your sexual desire because they nourish your feelings of sensuality.

What if you feel your sexual desire is low because of poor self-esteem or body image? Explore the body image exercises in Chapter 6. You can heal these attitudes by getting in touch with your body's unique beauties and strengths.

What if your desire for your partner has waned or you don't find him as attractive? The bonding and communication exercises in Chapters 3 and 12 will put you back in touch with your partner and his body, the nuances of your intimate relationship, and the qualities in your partner that drew you to him. They may also help you realize aspects of both of you that have grown and changed over time.

You may also boost your desire by encouraging your sensual and sexual potential.

- Try the self-touch exercises in Chapter 2 to learn about your own body.

- Increase your sexual fitness using the exercises in Chapter 4.

- The exercises that will probably make the biggest difference will be the sexual healing partner exercises in Chapter 5.

Ultimately, if you work through all the partner exercises you find in this book, including sexual healing intercourse, I guarantee your sexual desire will return.

Heightening Arousal

Do you have difficulty becoming aroused? Are you aware of your arousal sensations? Some women get concerned because they don't lubricate adequately or often. I have found that lubrication is not always a reliable sign of psychological or emotional arousal, which is a vital component of your desire. The amount of your lubrication can fluctuate with hormonal levels and age; it is a physical reflex that is connected to the touching of a particular vaginal area. You might lubricate without feeling emotionally turned on at all; conversely, you can be very turned on but not lubricate. You are better off using your feelings as an indication of your arousal rather than the wetness between your legs. If you do have difficulty lubricating, be sure to use an artificial lubricant so you stay comfortable.

If you have done exercises from other parts of this book, you've probably experienced new heights of arousal. The awareness, peaking and plateauing exercises in Chapter 6 are especially helpful for this.

If, after those exercises, you continue to experience difficulty getting aroused with your lover, try simply slowing down and savoring your sexual explorations. The solution for most women has been to slow down and enjoy more genital caressing and oral sex from their partner before beginning intercourse. Penetrating too soon can cause arousal problems for women. So can passively accepting whatever stimulation your partner wants to give you. So, another solution for arousal problems is to get active. You may receive a psychological boost from being in charge!

♀ Exercise ♂
Getting Active for Arousal

Have your lover remain passive. Ask him to lie on his back, close his eyes, and try not to move. Pretend his body is a playground or a toy for you to play with. Or, pretend he's asleep. Play with him, stroke, caress, lick, or suck on his body. Whatever you decide to do, do it slowly, sensuously, and without any pressure on either of you. If you want to climb on top of him and have intercourse, do. Chances are at some point in this exercise he won't be able to hold still any longer, and you two can revel in your sexual play together.

Increasing Orgasms

Difficulty having an orgasm during intercourse is one of the most common sexual complaints women have. In fact, some women have never felt an orgasm. I believe, however, that just about every woman has had an orgasm at some time in her life. She may have had one as a child, or in a dream or fantasy, but didn't recognize her feelings as orgasmic. More important, my experience is that every woman *can* be orgasmic. An orgasm is a basic body reflex, like yawning or sneezing, that is prompted by satisfactory arousal. The key is discovering your individual, orgasmic pathway.

As with desire, the type of stimulation that leads to orgasm and the delights of orgasm itself are unique for every woman. I encourage all women not to pressure themselves to have orgasm. What is important is that you open yourself to your orgasmic capacity in whatever ways feel good to you and your partner.

Some women strive for orgasm during intercourse not so much because it feels good, but because they wish to share this loving expression of intense arousal, vulnerability, and abandon with their partner. You will find through these exercises that sexual healing heightens your senses and deepens your intimacy.

A lot of women expect too much from orgasm, making it into a goal of life-changing proportions. Becoming orgasmic will and won't change your life: Your lovemaking will be more euphoric, your body will feel better, and your relationship and health will improve. But as far as I can tell, orgasm won't make you richer or thinner, make your kids behave, or keep your house clean. (It will certainly put you in a better mood . . . !)

Orgasms Come in All Colors, Shapes, and Sizes

Many women don't know what to expect during orgasm. When you have an orgasm, the muscles around your uterus and cervix spasm so that your abdomen flutters. You may expel some air from your vagina. Blood flows into your vaginal walls, creating pressure that causes a flow of lubrication. Your blood pressure, heart rate, and breathing all reach a peak. Your neck, arm, face, and leg muscles may spasm involuntarily, and tension in your PC muscle causes it to spasm shortly after. You may feel a tingling sensation in some parts of your body and a sensation of warmth that begins in your pelvis and spreads through to your chest, neck, and face. And you may flush.

During orgasm, your sympathetic nervous system and parasympathetic nervous system both work at the same time. Sexual energy builds up and is released rapidly, taking you to a state of relief, release, and sometimes, altered consciousness. Some women have "gushers" with their orgasms—female ejaculation, which is fluid expelled from the vagina. You may have heard that gushers are a myth, but they are real; they happen with intense stimulation of the G-spot, an extremely sensitive area in the upper front wall of the vagina.

This all sounds positively earth-shattering, doesn't it? But the reality for most women is that orgasms vary in intensity. Sometimes you may experience voluptuous, full-bodied orgasms and other times you might feel simple PC quivers and a mild, pleasant sensation. If you weren't paying attention you might even miss them. Some women make the mistake of expecting an earth-shattering event every time and are disappointed if they have a mild orgasm. As a result, over the years women have put incredible amounts of pressure on themselves to have orgasms. Women have actually undergone unnecessary surgery to remove the hood of the clitoris to make it more sensitive. I've even heard of a surgeon who operates on the PC muscle, supposedly to make it more sensitive.

If you have difficulty with orgasm, or if you have never had one, you *don't* need surgery. You are not unusual, and you don't have to settle for life without orgasm. After a program of sexual healing, you may reach new orgasmic heights.

♀ A Program ♂ for Increasing Orgasms

The first step in developing orgasmic potential is to explore your body and learn about your sexual responses. Lack of knowledge about your own response is the biggest single cause of inability to have orgasms. Don't depend on your partner to know what excites you. Deepen this knowledge yourself by doing all the sexual fitness, anxiety reduction, bonding, self-caress, arousal awareness, and peaking exercises described in Part One of this book.

You might consider buying a vibrator and experimenting with the different sensations and stimulation it can give you. It can help you find and explore the variety of delicious trigger points you may have missed until now. After exploring your arousal points, do the advanced healing exercises in Chapter 7 with your lover. Chances are, if you are a healthy woman, the basics of sexual healing will lead you to the brink of orgasm and beyond. Truthfully, you probably won't need anything else. The sexual healing exercises are fantastic for a woman who wants to explore her response, and they have worked for thousands of women.

If you do go all the way through this program and still are not orgasmic during intercourse, but would like to be, here are some secrets . . . .

♀ Exercise ♂
Masturbating with a Dildo

A woman's key to orgasm during intercourse is realizing the importance of the PC muscle spasm. Unless your PC muscle is in great shape, it is hard for it to spasm when you have something (anything) in your vagina. To practice becoming more orgasmic during intercourse, buy a dildo close to the size of your partner's penis and practice with it.

The Exercise   Give yourself a slow genital caress with the dildo. Keep the touch sensual, and remember to breathe and focus on your sensations. Insert the dildo, tease your PC muscle with it, and begin to peak. Squeeze and relax your PC muscle around the dildo, and caress your clitoris. Explore what feels good. When you reach the point of orgasm, insert the dildo just as your PC starts to spasm.

♀ Exercise ♂
Masturbating with Your Partner's Penis

After trying the previous exercise alone a few times, you are ready to do the same thing using your partner's penis.

The Exercise   Share a sensual genital caress or oral sex with your partner until he has an erection. Then lie on your back with your legs up and have him kneel between your legs. He can caress the opening of your vagina with his penis. Have him slowly tease your PC muscle by inserting only an inch and then withdrawing.

Have your partner alternate caressing your clitoris and stroking your PC muscle with his penis. After a few minutes of this, he can insert all the way and thrust deeply a few times. Because your PC muscle is tuned up from the previous exercise, it will begin to quiver and flutter around your partner's penis and will probably bring you to orgasmic spasms.

♀ Exercise ♂
Orgasm at Penetration

Many women think that the more time they spend in intercourse, the more likely they are to have an orgasm. Not surprisingly, a lot of men think this too. It is a myth. The truth is, if you are aroused enough during intercourse to have an orgasm, it will usually occur within about seven minutes. The next exercise shows that you don't need to spend extended amounts of time having intercourse in order to orgasm: you can learn to come within one or two strokes of penetration. The real secret to this exercise is peaking, not the penetration itself.

The Exercise Have your partner lie on his back and begin an oral genital caress with him. As he comes erect, slowly stimulate yourself by rubbing your clitoris and vaginal lips against his penis, but don't insert it. Peak up to levels seven and eight with this stimulation.

In between your peaks, have oral sex with your partner so he maintains high arousal levels.

Peak to level nine by slowly rubbing his penis on your clitoris and outside your vagina. Keep your leg muscles and PC muscle as relaxed as possible. Keep your eyes closed and increase your breathing. When you come to the brink of orgasm, open your eyes, take a deep breath, and thrust yourself all the way down on your partner's penis. You will likely reach orgasm within about five strokes.

Enjoy practicing this exercise until you can have an orgasm on the first stroke. If you peak yourself to level nine several times before penetration, rather than just once or twice, it increases your likelihood of having an immediate orgasm.

♀ Exercise ♂
Orgasm at Penetration
with the PC Muscle

You can also use your PC muscle to help you orgasm on your partner's first stroke. Do the exercise as described above, but when you sit on his penis, in addition to opening your eyes and taking a deep breath, slam your PC muscle shut around the shaft of your partner's penis. This will often trigger a powerful orgasm, especially if your PC muscle is already fluttering on the edge.

♀ Exercise ♂
The Bridge Maneuver

Although this sounds like something out of civil engineering, it is actually a gratifying way to bring your self-discovery together with your sexual partnership. This technique creates a psychological, behavioral bridge between your ability to orgasm when stimulating your clitoris yourself and your ability to orgasm with intercourse.

The Exercise Your partner lies on his back as you do a front caress and genital caress to arouse him. When he becomes erect, climb on top of him and begin peaking and plateauing, using his penis to pleasure yourself. As you reach high peaks and plateaus, stimulate your clitoris with your fingers. Masturbate to orgasm by stimulating your clitoris and allowing your partner's penis to stroke you. Notice the added sensations you feel with simultaneous masturbation and intercourse. With some practice, you will need less and less direct clitoral stimulation with your fingers, and your ability to have an orgasm will transfer to the stimulation of intercourse.

Variations   There are two variations of this exercise. Both work best if you are on top. Ask your partner to stimulate your clitoris with *his* hand instead of you doing it yourself. Or, either one of you can use a vibrator or dildo to stimulate your clitoris. You can also practice alternating peaks with the dildo, your hand, your partner's hand, and your partner's penis.

♀ Exercise ♂
Imitating Orgasm

Here is a very intense exercise to try if you are still having difficulty reaching orgasm. "Imitating orgasm" is not faking an orgasm to please your partner, to make him think you're having one when you're not. Instead, by imitating orgasm, you learn to fake your body into thinking you *are* having an orgasm. Often this triggers a real orgasm. This is most likely to help if you can peak up to a level nine but cannot seem to go over the edge.

The Exercise   Remember that the orgasmic response is a full body response, not something that occurs only in the genitals. At the moment of orgasm, your face contorts, your arms, neck, and legs spasm, and your PC muscle begins to contract. If you enact these body responses when you are at a level nine, there is a good chance that you will trigger an orgasm.

When you are making love with your partner and you reach level nine-plus, enact an orgasm: take a deep breath, suck in your lower abdomen, hunch your shoulders into the bed, thrust your pelvis up, open your eyes wide, and relax your PC muscle. This may trigger a real orgasm, which you will experience as a fluttering or spasming of the PC muscle.

Another way to do this is to wait until you are at the brink of orgasm and then slam your PC muscle shut instead of relaxing it. This can often trigger the necessary spasms.

A third alternative is to pretend you are having an orgasm and to act the way you think highly orgasmic women act. ("I'm ready for my close-up, Mr. De Mille.") Moan, flail your limbs, imitate an orgasm vocally, like Sally did in the movie *When Harry Met Sally.* Pretending that you are a highly arousable and orgasmic woman may allow you to practice orgasm techniques in a nonthreatening way, until you feel more comfortable with them.

All of these methods of triggering orgasm have several things in common. First, you learn to focus, breathe, and relax well enough to allow yourself to climb to exquisite, intense arousal. You learn to focus enough to avoid having any distracting thoughts when you do reach climactic levels of arousal.

Use these orgasm techniques not as ends in themselves but as ways to accustom yourself to having orgasms. As you become familiar with the power of these triggers, you will be able to use them with intercourse. As with any skill that involves learning complex patterns of behavior and combining them, the first few tries may feel artificial. After you practice these techniques for a while they become instinctual and your relaxation and arousal levels will lead you to fulfilling orgasms.

Healing Sexual Pain

There are two different types of sexual pain that women experience: vaginismus and dyspareunia. Both are physical sensations that are usually related to psychological pain.

Vaginismus

Vaginismus is a condition in which a woman's PC muscle, which surrounds the opening of the vagina, goes into a painful, uncontrolled spasm. As a result, the vagina tightens up and her partner cannot enter her. As with most sexual problems, vaginismus is caused by anxiety, which may stem from past sexual trauma, fear, lack of sexual knowledge, or abuse. The old treatment for vaginismus was to train a woman to insert a series of dilators, which are rods of graduated thickness, into her vagina to open it up. Now more effective, healing ways are used. Instead of using dilators, which are impersonal, you can use your own hands and your partner's hands to train yourself to relax your PC muscle. Here's how to begin.

- Use the PC muscle exercises in Chapter 4 to gain control over your reflexes, paying special attention to the relaxation phase in between PC squeezes.

- Then try the self-caress and genital caress from Chapter 2, to become familiar and comfortable with your body. If you are not able to insert a finger inside your vagina, don't worry, just caress the outside.

- Next, repeat the exercises for anxiety and depression from Chapter 6.

- Use the bonding and other partner exercises in Chapters 3 and 5 to draw on your partner's healing power, but stop at the genital caress.

If you have vaginismus, you may have to modify the above exercises a bit to stay comfortable. For example, you may want to break an exercise into smaller parts and only work through a part of the exercise at each session. Also, you should make sure your PC muscle is relaxed during every exercise. If your PC muscle is not relaxed or if it starts to tense up, stop the exercise and go back to a previous exercise with which you felt comfortable. If you are not aware whether your PC muscle is tightening up during a partner exercise, ask your partner to help you. When you have worked through this program, try the following penetration exercises.

♀ Exercise ♂
Finger Penetration for Vaginismus

This is a special exercise for you when you reach the stage where you can do the genital caress by yourself. Slowly caress your clitoris and vaginal lips using the sensate focus techniques. Breathe and relax. Relax your PC muscle and try to insert the tip of your little finger into your vagina just one-half inch. Tighten your PC muscle around your fingertip and then relax it. Now see if you can insert it an inch. Tighten, and relax again. Keep going with this until you can insert every finger on each hand all the way in. If at any time you feel pain, don't push yourself, but back up to a stage you feel comfortable with.

♀ Exercise ♂
Penetration with Your Partner's Fingers

This exercise brings in the healing energies of your partner. It is essentially the same as the exercise above, but instead of using your own fingers you use your partner's fingers.

Lie down in a comfortable position and have your partner lie next to you. After caressing yourself with your hand and his fingers, take his hand and gradually insert each finger from the smallest to the largest, tightening and relaxing your PC muscle at each stage. Your partner should keep his hand totally relaxed, because the important thing is that you are in charge of the depth and timing of any penetration.

♀ Exercise ♂
Penetration with a Dildo

Buy a dildo that appeals to you and that is about halfway between the size of a finger and your partner's penis. Make yourself comfortable, and then follow the steps of the penetration exercise above using the dildo instead of your partner's fingers. Remember to breathe, relax, and focus on positive, sensual feelings.

♀ Exercise ♂
Penetration with Your
Partner's Flaccid Penis

Follow the exercise for flaccid insertion in Chapter 10, but insert your partner's penis one-half inch at a time instead of all at once. Then progress to doing this exercise with his partially erect penis and, eventually, with a full erection. Then try the exercise in other positions in addition to side-to-side. The important thing is that *you* stay in charge of the timing, depth, and angle of penetration until you are comfortable having your partner do it. At that point, you will be ready to try some of the advanced sexual healing exercises from Chapter 7 and the types of healing intercourse from Chapter 8.

Vaginismus can be a frustrating condition and you may feel it takes forever to treat, but be patient and take small steps—you will reach your goal of sexual healing intercourse. And the rewards are great.

Dyspareunia

Dyspareunia is psychological pain during intercourse. If you experience pain during intercourse, you should first rule out all possible medical causes, which may include menstrual problems, tumors, ovarian cysts, venereal disease, pelvic infections, endometriosis, or an injury such as a pulled muscle or torn ligament. It is unlikely that a physical abnormality of the vagina is causing your problem, although there have been cases of septate vagina (a split vagina with a membrane down the middle) and women born without vaginas or with vaginas only an inch or so deep.

If you have been to a physician and ruled out physical causes, it is likely your pain during intercourse has a psychological origin. This is especially likely if you experience sharp, piercing vaginal pain during intercourse, since the vagina does not actually have the nerve endings to feel that type of pain.

The first step to healing dyspareunia is to get comfortable with the basic sexual healing exercises that I recommend for everybody: the self-touch, bonding, partner exercises, and sexual fitness exercises. When doing caresses, particularly genital caresses, don't continue anything that causes you pain. After you have begun to develop a healing momentum with these exercises, try the following.

♀ Exercise ♂
Exploring Your Vagina

During a genital caress, insert your finger into your vagina as far as is comfortable. When you reach a point where you feel pain, back off and only do the caress up to the point where the pain starts. (Remember, if you cannot insert a finger at all, you have vaginismus, not dyspareunia).

The next time you do this exercise, use a small dildo instead of your finger. Insert the dildo to the point where you are afraid you might feel pain. Relax your PC muscle and see if you can insert a little farther. Remember to breathe slowly and deeply, and keep your legs and all other muscles relaxed. Make a mark on the dildo to show how far you inserted it. Each time you repeat the exercise, see if you can insert the dildo a little farther without pain.

Your goal is to become comfortable with penetration, so you can penetrate without pain.

♀ Exercise ♂
Penetration with Your
Partner's Penis (for Sexual Pain)

Have your partner lie on his back and stimulate him with a genital caress and oral sex until he has an erection. Then, caress plenty of lubrication onto your genital area, climb on top of your partner, and slowly insert his penis a half-inch at a time. If you reach a point where you feel pain, stop. Relax your PC muscle and keep going as long as you are comfortable. Slowly thrust all the way up and down on the penis as long as it doesn't hurt. Stay in control of all the thrusting—your partner should remain passive, without moving.

Repeat intercourse in this way until you are comfortable with your partner starting to move. He can begin by slightly, sensuously rolling his hips.

When that becomes comfortable, try changing positions and exploring some of the more advanced sexual healing exercises from Chapter 7 and the types of sexual healing intercourse from Chapter 8.

If Your Partner Has Arousal Problems, Orgasm Problems, or Sexual Pain

If you are the partner of a woman who is working to heal her sexual problems, you can help a great deal by sharing some of these exercises with her. There are two things you can do to help her: first, learn to receive. This is the biggest gift you can give her, because it will be just as healing for her to be active—if not more so—as it is for you to do something for her. You may need to let go of the "I can be a hero who solves the problem" role and let her explore things for herself.

Another thing you can do to help heal your partner is to concentrate on the touches you two share. Channel your attention and your affection into that touch, and give it healing power. When you have intercourse, picture yourself caressing her vagina with your penis. Instead of thrusting hard and fast for your own pleasure, really feel every inch of her vagina, concentrate on healing it, and experience pleasure together.

When to Get Professional Help

As always, if you work through these exercises and you are still having problems, you should see a professional who can help you get motivated. This is especially important if sexual abuse or trauma in your past is preventing you from experiencing the healing touch.

Chapter 12

Lovemaking to Heal Your Relationship

he advanced exercises in this chapter are aimed at nourishing the intangible strengths of a loving relationship: the powers of intimacy, commitment, trust, mutuality, and respect.

I am sure you have learned a lot about your relationship from working through some of these exercises, especially the bonding exercises in Chapter 3. But your ability to experience intimacy, mutuality, and commitment may be thwarted by what I call the "Three As": abuse, addiction, and adultery.

If your relationship suffers from one of these significant wounds, you and your partner may need professional help to heal, but experience has taught me that the sexual healing exercises are powerful enough to help you start dealing with, and healing from, these wounds. Loving relationships are surprisingly resilient, especially when lovers are given the means to overcome traumas. I have seen some relationships severely threatened by these traumas *and* I have seen the power of sexual healing help couples overcome them. What follows is a simplified discussion of the Three As, with suggestions for areas of possible solutions. Each issue is worthy of specific, in-depth discussion, and several good books have been written on them. If you are having difficulty dealing with any of the Three As, I encourage you to seek a counselor's help. For further reading, I suggest you go to the library or a bookstore and pick out three or four books that appeal to you. If you wish to have more emotional support, most local newspapers have sections that list anonymous support groups.

Abuse

Abuse can be physical, emotional or sexual. It may have occurred in the past, or it can be a factor in a present relationship. Sexual abuse, especially if you experienced it during childhood, can create a huge schism between the experiences of having sex and making love. Also, during sexual intimacy the abused person may suffer flashbacks of the childhood trauma.

Carol sought the help of a male surrogate partner to deal with her inability to become aroused and have an orgasm with a part- ner. Whenever she approached orgasm during arousal, she felt her- self shutting down and becoming distracted. In work with the surrogate partner, Carol revealed that she had severe psychological conflicts related to a recent, abusive relationship. Every episode of intercourse brought up anxieties associated with that relationship. For Carol, successfully healing from her experiences required talk- ing through the abuse with her therapist and working with the surrogate partner on the distractions and anxiety as they came up in sexual settings. With sexual healing, Carol found peace of mind and got back in touch with her body.

The sexual healing exercises are perfect for helping you heal the split between having sex and making love, but you will have to take them at a slow pace—and that is *fine*. It is vital for your healing to remember that you will be in control of the boundaries of any exercise, and the exercise will only go as far as you want it to. The exercises in Chapters 2 and 5 will be especially helpful, and will reintroduce you to the dynamic powers of touch and its healthy, healing potential.

In addition to sexual healing, one of the things I have seen make a difference in the lives of abuse victims is writing. Dr. James Pennebaker outlines an effective technique in his book, *Opening Up*. He describes how writing about a traumatic event in your past can help you confront and deal with that event, and gives you strate- gies and steps to do so.

Amazingly, writing about a traumatic event has the additional, wonderful benefit of boosting your immune system. The effects have been demonstrated, but how it works has not been proven. The hypothesis is that repressing a trauma, whether consciously or unconsciously, is highly stressful, which decreases the immune response. Writing about trauma provides a healthy outlet for coping and reduces stress.

Addiction

Addiction doesn't refer simply to alcoholism, drug addiction, or even sexual addiction. It encompasses all compulsive behaviors with similar natures, including compulsive shopping, eating, or gambling. Compulsive behaviors are behaviors that control you, sidestepping your rational will and interfering with the course and fulfillment of your life. These compulsions are generally driven by anxiety and often escalate; for example, a drug addict often needs more and more of a drug to get the same high.

Your intimate relationship with your partner may be marred by a sexual compulsion. This can take a number of forms: one of you is attracted to inappropriate partners (such as children or inanimate objects), or displays excessive frequencies of normal behaviors (such as compulsive masturbation or nymphomania).

The sexual healing exercises are good for compulsive behaviors for a couple of reasons. First, compulsion is created and reinforced by a vicious circle of emotions and behavior: anxiety leads to the behavior, and the behavior induces momentary relaxation. Because so many of the sexual healing exercises teach relaxation, they can help compulsive people reduce the initial anxiety that feeds their compulsive behavior. When the compulsion is less strong, they can work on relearning healthier, and ultimately more comfortable, behavior.

People often develop sexual compulsions because they have no concept of normal sexual behavior or a normal sexual relationship.

The sexual healing exercises can provide that dose of normality, especially the exercises in Chapters 3, Setting the Stage for a Healing Relationship, Chapter 5, How to Be a Sexual Healer—Beginning Exercises, and Chapter 6, Using Lovemaking to Heal Emotional and Mental Problems. I also believe that it is important for people with addiction issues to work on these issues first and continuously.

Adultery

On the one hand, I believe that jealousy can poison a relationship. Most people I have met are entirely too jealous and possessive. Their paranoia or need to control their partner reflects their own self-esteem and lack of trust and respect for their partner, their relationship, and themselves. It keeps them from truly enjoying the richness of a loving partnership. On the other hand, some people abuse their partner's trust by having extramarital affairs.

What constitutes infidelity needs to be defined by the two of you in your particular relationship. Love, promise, and commitment are the cornerstones of an intimate partnership. But how they are defined and how they fit together can only be decided— mutually—by the two of you. I have known couples who considered each other unfaithful if they went out to lunch with a member of the opposite sex. I have known others who said to each other, "Feel free to have sex with other people. Just don't fall in love with them." Most of us fall somewhere in between. What is important is that you both agree on the standards of your relationship and promise to live by them.

I do believe that the lifelong healing relationship detailed in this book is most powerful and most healing if it is monogamous. For most couples, extramarital sex creates a wound in the relationship because of the betrayal of trust. In my experience, however, these wounds can be healed and relationships can become strong again, especially if the affair was a short one. By all means, use the exercises in this book to help yourselves get over the anger and re-bond with each other. The exercises in Chapter 3, Setting the Stage for a Healing Relationship, will be especially helpful for you.

If there is adultery in your relationship's history, you may discover unresolved issues surrounding it are at the root of sexual difficulties you two have. For example, *Steve* sought professional help for sexual problems—he had difficulties with erections and had been unable to ejaculate for years. It turned out that in the early years of his marriage his wife had an affair, and twenty years later Steve was still unable to forgive her. Not surprisingly, Steve's inability to ejaculate dated from that time. In therapy Steve tackled his emotional issues. In the bedroom, he relaxed and he and his wife worked to strengthen their intimacy.

On the other hand, compulsively having affairs and using them to manipulate your partner is severely abusive and requires professional help.

If your relationship is marred by any of the Three As, you could have the best healing intentions in the world but they will not help unless you are both inspired to change your situation. For sexual healing to occur, the healing intentions must be mutual.

Deepening Your Intimacy

There are a couple of different ways to increase the intimacy in your relationship. These are simple, yet are often overlooked. In the rat race of everyday life we need to cherish the feelings that brought us together by continuing to play with each other. We can also honor these feelings and maintain our intimacy through verbal communication. Some of the following exercises appeared in my book, *Sexual Pleasure,* in the chapter "Strengthening the Bonds that Sustain You." So if you like them and would like to learn more, you might want to check out *Sexual Pleasure.*

Play

A lot of our unstructured lovemaking serves the same function for us that play does for kids. It lets us relax and take the pressure off ourselves. It is dynamic, creative, expressive, and unself-conscious. Unlike most activities in our adult lives, lovemaking isn't goal-oriented (or at least it shouldn't be). And it *is* true that the family that plays together stays together. If you and your partner wish to enrich your relationship, one of the things you can do is to play sports together or indulge in other games you enjoy. Or, the two of you could try a couple of these romantically playful exercises.

♀ Exercise ♂
Sensuous Shower

The sensuous shower is a whole-body caress that takes place in the shower. The purpose of the sensuous shower is not to get clean (though you probably will), but to enjoy your own body and your partner's body in a different way.

There are a number of ways to savor a sensuous shower. You can share any of the caresses you have learned in this book, caressing each other's face, chest, back, genitals. You can include oral sex. If you like, you can alternate taking active and passive roles. Or, you can make this exercise a mutual caress, and caress each other at the same time. Don't forget that you can caress with all the different parts of your body, not just your fingers.

Try using a liquid bath soap or fragrant bath gel, and caress any parts of your partner's body that feel good. When you caress, touch for your own pleasure. Focus on the silky sensations of your partner's wet skin and hair. When you receive a caress, concentrate on exactly where you are being touched, just as you would during any sensate focus exercise.

If you become aroused during the caress, simply allow yourself to experience the arousal. Don't try to heighten your arousal or push it away. Relax and enjoy the feelings of your partner caressing you and the water beating down on your skin. If you have an erection, ejaculation, or orgasm, welcome it.

After the shower, pat each other dry with warm towels and a loving touch.

The sensuous shower can be a relaxing prelude to healing exercises such as the genital and oral caress. If you prefer baths rather than showers, dim the lights in the bathroom, light a few candles, and take a bath together using scented bath oils or soaps.

♀ Exercise ♂
Tom Jones Dinner

Many of us gobble our food or eat while doing other things. We fail to take the time to enjoy the simple, sensuous aspects of eating. Now here is your opportunity!

The Tom Jones Dinner is named for the incredibly indulgent eating scene in the movie of the same name. We did this exercise as part of surrogate training, and here is what happened: Everyone in the class (ten to twelve people) brought some type of food that could be eaten with the hands. We spread a sheet out on the floor and laid out the foods beautifully. We were all nude (this was the 70s) and there were three rules: no feeding yourself, no talking, and no using utensils. Everybody fed each other. Some of these dinners got pretty wild, with people eating food off each others' bodies. However, the point of the dinner was not to have a wild food orgy, but to learn to enjoy the purely sensuous aspects of eating, free from the restraints of table manners.

You can create a delectable Tom Jones Dinner at home for you and your partner. First, choose some sensuous foods. You might consider fruit (especially juicy ones, such as oranges and peaches), hors d'oeuvres such as cheese and crackers, any meat that can be pulled off the bone, and anything messy that can be licked off fingers and body parts. In general, anything that is creamy or juicy will feel especially good in your mouth. For beverages, serve wine or champagne, sparkling water, or fruit juice.

Arrange the food on a sheet to protect your carpeting and furniture. Take off your clothes. Relax and caress each other if you need a transition, then begin to feed each other. Go slowly, just as you would in a caressing exercise. Eat with the goal of feeling every sensation as the food passes your lips and through your mouth. Watch your partner eat. Place food on your partner's body and slowly lick it off, or offer food to your partner on yours. If you want a drink, take a drink and then, with a kiss, share it with your partner.

Finish the Tom Jones Dinner by washing each other off with warm, wet towels or taking a sensuous shower.

♀ Exercise ♂
Act Like an Animal

Part of being intimate is recognizing that lovemaking is playful and doesn't have to be serious, that you can really "let your hair down" with your partner. Sex is a basic animal activity and some-times you may want to do it just to express that animal urge. This exercise is based on one from my recent book, *Talk Sexy to the One You Love*, called "Wild Thing." I used to call it "Quest For Fire," and have elaborated on it here.

One of you will be passive while the other is active. The passive partner lies on his or her back. The active person then uses the partner's body to indulge in and gratify his or her "animal urges."

When you are the active partner, lick, stroke, and suck your partner as if you were an animal. Make a lot of animal noises while you do this, such as grunting and moaning. Rub yourself against different parts of your partner's body. Groom your partner. If you are a woman and your partner has an erection, you squat on top of him and thrust up and down. If you are a man, you push your partner's legs back and penetrate, or roll her over and enter her from behind. (Don't forget to bay at the moon when you're done.)

Be creative and have fun with this, but don't do anything that might hurt your partner.

Verbal Intimacy

Besides play, one of the things that will enrich your emotional relationship is to learn to talk to each other more comfortably. To learn some fun, sexy word games, try the exercises in *Talk Sexy to the One You Love*. Or, if you are still a little tongue-tied, try this basic exercise.

♀ Exercise ♂
Observe, Reflect, Ask

This is a basic communication exercise that can be adapted and used during lovemaking. A lot of couples, regardless of how long they have been together, do great with the touching aspects of the sensate focus exercises but are uncomfortable communicating verbally during lovemaking. Yet this kind of intimacy can bring you great pleasure, both physical and emotional. This exercise is especially helpful for those of you who have a difficult time saying *anything* during sex.

One of you will be active while the other is passive. Decide together what caresses the active person will do.

The active partner should caress for about half an hour, going from the back caress to the front caress, to the genital caress, to oral sex. As the passive partner, stop your partner at some point into the exercise when you really enjoy what is going on. First, *observe* to yourself, "She's stroking my penis in a way that I really find pleasurable." Then *reflect* on that thought with your partner, repeating it as an "I" statement: "I really like the way you are caressing my penis." Then *ask* your partner to keep doing that caress for a few minutes: "Please caress my penis this way for a few more minutes."

During a half-hour exercise, observe and ask for several different things. Then switch roles.

Mutuality

Here are some very advanced exercises to help you both feel you are on the same road, traveling in the same direction. They call on the peaking and plateauing techniques you have learned and create incredible feelings of connected energy.

♀ Exercise ♂
Mutual Orgasm

I am sure you have heard the phrase "simultaneous orgasm," which refers to couple having an orgasm at the same time during intercourse. In sexology, for a long time simultaneous orgasm was touted as the be-all and end-all of lovemaking. It eventually fell out of favor with sex therapists because many of them realized this point of view puts too much pressure on couples, especially men who have premature ejaculation problems and women who have difficulty coming to orgasm during intercourse.

Some of us, however, have not given up on the rare potential of simultaneous orgasm, which I prefer to call "mutual orgasm" because it reflects so much more than simply two orgasms happening at the same time. The phrase *mutual orgasm* also reflects the idea that each lover enjoys their partner's orgasm as well as his or her own. With the techniques in this book, especially peaking and plateauing, you and your partner can know so much about each other's response that you will be able to have mutual orgasms.

The Exercise Mutual orgasm is an outgrowth of the sensate focus intercourse from Chapter 8. You begin with some unstructured foreplay or focusing caresses to awaken your senses. Then decide who will be on top. Bring your bodies together in an intercourse position in which you are face to face. Whoever is on top controls the speed of the thrusting and should start as slowly as possible.

As you roll through slow, sensuous thrusting, peak together up through levels six, seven, and eight. Relax, breathe, and focus on the sensations in the penis and vagina. Men, think of yourself as caressing the vagina with your penis. Women, think of yourself as caressing your partner's penis with the walls of your vagina. Keep your motion shared and mutual as you thrust together and slide apart. Look at each other as you move. If you've done many peaking and plateauing exercises, you are probably very aware of your own and your partner's arousal levels. Remember that the best cues for your partner's arousal level are heart rate and breathing.

When the person on top climbs to the brink of orgasm, the other should follow. As you plunge into orgasm, take a deep breath, relax your body, open your eyes wide, and look into your partner's eyes. With practice you will find that you have the ability either to hold back slightly until your partner is ready or to accelerate your arousal slightly to match your partner.

If you frequently experience mutual orgasm with your partner, you may think this is as good as lovemaking gets. But what if you could experience multiple orgasms together? Read on.

♀ Exercise ♂
Multiple Orgasms for Men

In *How to Make Love All Night* I wrote extensively about this delicious experience, but I would like to explain the basics of it here because, for a couple, it is really the "icing on the cake" of mutual orgasm.

Contrary to popular expectation it is possible for men to have multiple orgasms the same way women do. To learn how, you have to realize that orgasm and ejaculation are two different body processes. An orgasm is a full body response that includes spasms of the long muscles of the body, rapid heart rate, rapid breathing, and an intense feeling of pleasure and release. Ejaculation is a localized genital phenomenon that occurs when the PC muscle spasms and forces semen out of the penis.

Every man can become multiply orgasmic by learning to let his body go over into the sensations of orgasm while delaying or withholding ejaculation. You can do this by being intensely aware of the sensations that happen right at your point of ejaculatory inevitability or the "point of no return," and keeping yourself from going over that point. Because you don't ejaculate, you can maintain your erection and continue making love, during which time you may go on to have one or several more orgasms. Many men especially enjoy having an ejaculation with their final orgasm.

Becoming multiply orgasmic holds several benefits for men. By understanding the powers of orgasmic potential, you gain insight into your partner's response and it becomes easier for the two of you to communicate about sexual matters. Also, women whose partners become multiply orgasmic delight in the sharing of this very special experience.

The Exercise   There are numerous, detailed exercises in *How to Make Love All Night,* but try beginning with a preliminary exercise here. Some men have learned this in just a few sessions.

First, bring yourself to orgasmic potential by trying it alone while doing a genital caress. Peak yourself up to levels six, seven, and eight, and then do plateaus at eight and nine. When you reach that split-second before your PC starts to spasm, squeeze the PC muscle as tight as you can for five to ten seconds, open your eyes, take a few deep breaths, and relax all your other muscles. You will have an unusual sensation in which you have an orgasm but don't ejaculate. If you ejaculate a little bit, it just means you need to practice your timing.

Next, try the same exercise when making love with your partner. Most men prefer making love in this way from the kneeling position. I find that the men who learn this the most quickly are those who are able to get rid of their performance attitude and make love just because they enjoy it and their partners.

♀ Exercise ♂
Multiple Orgasms for Women

For women, the way to trigger multiple orgasms is similar to the Plateauing with Intercourse exercise in Chapter 8. Multiple orgasms may be very strong, quiet, somewhere in-between, or a combination of all these.

You can have multiple orgasms in any position. Many women find that being on top is more active and gives them more ability to control their stroking and arousal. Other women find that having their partners kneel while they lie on their back provides more stimulation, particularly of the G-spot. I encourage you to try different positions and different types of orgasms. You may want to try multiple orgasms alone first, with genital caresses or a dildo, before trying them with your partner.

The Exercise Peak to levels four, five, and six. Then, plateau at level seven with breathing, pelvic movements, a PC squeeze, or switching focus. When you peak to levels eight and nine, instead of plateauing, let yourself wash over into an orgasm. Then continue stimulation and peaking until you reach another orgasm. The more you are able to let yourself go and revel in your sensation, the more you will be likely to have multiple orgasms.

Strengthening Your Commitment

Ultimately, you and your partner reinforce commitment to your relationship by the nature of your day-to-day lives together, and you strengthen commitment by honoring each other. There are several ways in which sexual healing techniques will deepen your feelings of commitment. By joining together to explore the healing power of your sexual love, you and your partner are reinforcing your commitment. There is no special exercise to work on commitment—you do it with the exercises in this book.

The important things to remember are: When you make a date or a plan to do a particular exercise, keep the date as much as you are able. Both you and your partner have looked forward to this, and anticipation is necessary for your success. Also, decide what exercise you will do in advance, talk about it, and as much as possible stick with the original plan. Try not to change your mind. Finally, during any exercise, stay within the bounds of the exercise that you have agreed to. If you do this consistently, you and your partner will deepen your trust, or can rebuild some of the trust you may have lost because of problems of addiction or infidelity. Your commitment to keeping those small promises will build your trust step by step.

Assessing Your Relationship Needs

Ask each other, "what are the problem in our relationship?" Then, separately, write down a list of things that bother you about your relationship. Include everything from the big things to the little things.

Next, look over your lists together and circle the things that have common themes, such as trust, intimacy, commitment, communication, respect, or mutuality. Circle them and label them in whatever way makes the most sense to the two of you.

From this list you should be able to discern the areas you would like to improve in your relationship, and you can use appropriate sexual healing exercises to work on them.

For example, let's say your list includes many things with a "we never do anything together" theme. This is a mutuality problem and will best be solved by exercises done together—everything from the basics to advanced peaking, plateauing, and intercourse. The more mutual and shared the outcome, the better it will be for you.

As another example, let's say your list includes a lot of things to the effect of "Our relationship is okay, but I just don't feel as close as I used to." Bingo! This sounds like Chapter 3—Setting the Stage for a Healing Relationship—will suit your needs.

Is There Anything Else?

Sure, I'd like to keep going and share with you every sex therapy exercise ever invented . . . but you know your relationship better than anyone else does. And with the knowledge of sexual healing under your belt, you are at the stage where you will know what you need to work on and how best to do it. At this stage it is time for you and your partner to design your own, unique exercises. Talk about what your relationship needs, and then pull together appropriate elements from previous chapters and make it happen! For sexual healing to grow and take effect it must come from the heart and from both partners' mutual healing intentions. Trust that you now have the instincts and insight to come together in this vital, healing way.

I'd like to make one last point about relationships, because too often we simply give it lip service. Honor and respect are not just words. They are the cornerstones of the life you build together as spouses and partners. If you read any interview with couples who have been together for fifty years or more, they will all mention these two words.

Respect is like self-esteem, but is directed at your partner. You feel the same about your partner as you do about yourself. Respect goes one step farther than the Golden Rule, "Do unto others as you would have others do unto you." Respect says, "I will treat my partner not only the way I wish to be treated, but the way I would treat myself."

Without honor and respect, your relationship can fall prey to the "natural disasters" in life. But you must work for these qualities; they don't often develop easily. They begin in your home with specific actions. They affect your expectations and your reactions. Even if you are angry with your partner or feel the need to criticize something, you can do this in a way that shows honor and respect to your partner.

Strong, lasting relationships are built on a foundation of love for each other, joy and playfulness, sexual fulfillment, commitment and trust, mutual honor, respect for each person's body and individuality, and the promise to carry on. My wish for you and your partner is that your relationship begins with these qualities and continues to grow in richness, depth, and dimension.

Chapter 13

Spiritual Healing
through Lovemaking

mar Sharif once said, "Making love? It is a communion with a woman. The bed is a holy table. There I find passion—and purification." Indeed, making love in a committed, intimate mutual relationship can open up a vast spiritual dimension in which you two connect with each other and with something larger than either—or both—of you.

I am not religious and I don't consider myself particularly spiritual, but I *do* know that you are missing something in life if you don't have a feeling for the transpersonal, even if the connection you feel is simply with nature. I have kept this chapter until last because it is an introduction to another dimension of sexuality—sacred sexuality—and some of you may relate to it while others may not. I encourage you to explore what this dimension can hold for you and your partner.

You may have already experienced the transpersonal or transcendental element of lovemaking. For example, have you ever felt an altered state of consciousness, in which everything looked clearer or brighter, after uniquely passionate sex? Physically we explain this altered state of consciousness as resulting from the combination of hyperventilation and endorphin release, but that shortchanges the profound effects such sexual connection can have on us. Many couples find sexual union is a way to realize their connection with a higher power, whether that power for them is God or the goddess, nature or goodness.

Sexuality in Religious Traditions

Most religious traditions have recognized the power of lovemaking and tie it into their cosmology, or theory of the universe. The Judeo-Christian religions honor the Bible, which includes the Song of Songs, a lavish and beautiful poem that celebrates the eroticism of heterosexual lovemaking. The Orthodox Jewish traditions refer to the Kabbalah, which also contains erotic passages. The Islamic religion also includes erotic love poems. Buddhist, Taoist, and Hindu traditions all feature artwork depicting sexual scenes, and they include a focus on how sexual energy is a way to transcend this world. Have you ever seen pictures of some of the Hindu temple carvings in India and Thailand? They are frankly erotic, often illustrating copulation between gods and mortals.

For some people, however, the idea that an organized religion could contain a tradition of sacred sex is very threatening. So many of us have had negative upbringings in restrictive religious traditions in which sexuality was forbidden rather than celebrated. Many of us learned to avoid sex because our religious background taught us to associate the body and its sexual impulses with shame and guilt.

For example, I grew up in the Catholic tradition and sex was strictly forbidden (and not even discussed) until you were married. Upon marriage, suddenly lovemaking became so special that it was a gift from God, a sacrament that reflected the marriage of Christ and the church. This was a challenging belief for my friends and me to understand and come to terms with, particularly as teenagers who were discovering our sexuality, often in the backs of cars! It was very difficult for us to relate to sexuality in a sacramental sense when our entire lives up to that point had been governed by a "don't ask, don't tell" policy.

Understanding the historical roles of sexuality in our religious tradition can help heal the disjunction we might feel between spirituality and sexuality. Sexual healing can make it possible to heal these attitudes and allow your sexual relationship to enrich you spiritually as well as physically and emotionally.

♀ Exercise ♂
Spiritual and Erotic Reading

If you are a member of an organized religion, find out what your religious tradition has to say about using lovemaking as an expression of your spirituality and your relationship with the deity. Whether your religious background is Christian, Moslem, Goddess, nature worship, the "old religion," or something else, you can find readings around sacred sexuality. On a special night, take some of the erotic and/or spiritual writings in your tradition and read them aloud to each other.

♀ Exercise ♂
Foot Bath and Caress

This exercise is not only sensual, it is also symbolic of humility and service. You may do this clothed or in the nude, however you and your partner feel comfortable and close.

Before You Begin   You will need two towels, a basin large enough for a person's feet, liquid soap, lotion, and hot water.

The Exercise   To begin, the passive partner sits in a chair with his or her feet on the floor. The bath itself only includes the feet and ankles. The active partner fills the basin with warm water and gently places the passive partner's feet in the water.

Add the liquid soap and caress your partner's feet in the water. The foot bath is like any other sensate focus exercise. Use a light, caressing touch, not massage. Bathe one foot at a time, finding out how the different areas of the foot feel as you bathe them. Stroke the ankles, the arches, and the tender underside of the toes. Although you touch for your own pleasure, believe me, your partner will like this one! As you touch your partner, draw the healing mindset around the two of you.

When you are done bathing both your partner's feet, lift them from the basin one at a time, pat them dry, and wrap them in separate towels. Put aside the basin, then take one foot from the towel, warm up some lotion in your palms and caress the foot with lotion. Again, caress for your own pleasure. I usually bathe each foot for about five minutes and then caress each foot for five to ten minutes.

As the passive person during the foot bath and caress, the only thing you need to do is relax and enjoy. Allow yourself to be pampered. Relax your feet and let them hang from your legs. Your partner will lift them into the basin for you—you don't need to help. Can you feel the warm tingles from your feet stream up your legs?

♀ Exercise ♂
The Five Senses

In this exercise you use religious or spiritual symbols, such as earth, air, fire, and water, to gather just the right combination of elements that will engage all five of your partner's senses in lovemaking. Each of you can take turns being the bearer of delights.

The Exercise   When it is your turn, prepare your room for lovemaking with things that will feed the five senses. For example, you could choose a jasmine-scented candle to appeal to your partner's sense of smell, wear something sexy that is pleasing to the eye, and play some soulful music on the stereo. Then you could uncork your partner's favorite wine to stimulate the taste buds, and use your fingertips or palms to caress his or her skin. Make sure not to have too many things going on. One stimulus for each sense is enough.

When you are receiving the five senses (your partner has prepared the room), try to empty yourself of thoughts and open yourself to your senses. Focus on each sense, one at a time, then experience them as a whole.

This exercises allows you to combine sensate focus with the sensual pleasures you know your partner likes, and also make a symbolic and real connection between lovemaking with your partner and outward symbols of your spiritual tradition such as candles and wine.

♀ Exercise ♂
Body Decoration

Before You Begin　Buy some body paints that are suitable for use on skin. You can find these at a bath shop, an adult store, or through a catalog.

The Exercise　Try this in your bathtub or shower, or a secluded, private area outside if you have one. Undress each other and offer each other your body. Your body may become a canvas for spiritual, sacred expression, or a part of you that your partner is honoring. Each of you takes turns painting your partner's body with reverence. You may wish to paint symbols that mean something to both of you. Or designs that celebrate your body and body parts. You can turn this into a ritual, if you wish. When you are both painted, do whatever you are inspired to do—if the paints are edible, lick them off.

♀ Exercise ♂
Symbolic Dinner

The breaking of bread and sharing of food can be a symbolic ceremony. For example, the Jewish tradition of Passover remembers the Jews' flight out of Egypt; each food served at a Passover supper holds symbolic meaning.

Have you and your partner gone through difficult times? Are there special times of rejoicing? Do you cherish special aspects of your relationship? Share a symbolic dinner that honors your history or sets the stage for your future together.

The Exercise   Again, consider this exchange a ritual or ceremony. Plan it in advance so it has a structure. Serve special foods that remind you of some aspect in your relationship or symbolize some aspect of your love. Make up a dialogue to go along with serving the food. For example, "As I'm pouring this wine, it reminds me of our wedding, when we shared this same wine with our close friends . . . . " Alternately, you could prepare some readings to accompany each dish or course.

♀ Exercise ♂
Personal Altars

Practitioners of some Eastern religions often keep altars in their homes. They light candles or incense and meditate and pray before their altar. Some Christians do this also. In a similar way, try honoring your relationship.

You could make your bedroom, or another private room in your house, a shrine to your relationship, using pictures and symbols. Here are some ideas (just call me the Martha Stewart of sexual healing!):

Choose artwork with healing imagery such as mandalas (Hindu symbols of the universe), spirals (symbols of an inner journey), or suns (symbols of life). Use statues and paintings that symbolize male and female fertility. Play classical or New Age music, or music that mimics the heart's rhythms. For aromas, scent the room with essential oils of rosemary, lavender, eucalyptus, ginger, or clove. Make sure your room can have plenty of sunlight and fresh air. All of these will contribute to your spiritual well-being.

Tantra

The religious or sacred tradition that has the most to say about making love is tantra—a form of yoga done in couples. The tantric cosmology features a whole theory of the universe created by the male and female forces. The universe springs from the union of the god Shiva (pure consciousness) and his consort Shakti (pure energy). The difference between most forms of yoga that you may be familiar with and tantra is that most yoga preaches asceticism—getting away from the worldly and the material, whereas tantra teaches how to reach the sublime by "debasing" oneself—becoming material, corporal, and earthy. The most profound way to do this is by having sex.

In tantra, the man and woman making love symbolize the male and female forces that created and power the universe. The male and female genitals are revered objects of worship. Tantra includes exercises, positions, rituals, and sexual postures that all have meaning in the tantric belief system. I hosted a *Playboy* video called "A Guide to Tantric Lovemaking" that shows modern couples how to do some of these exercises and practices, some of which are quite weird by modern standards. For example, one of the tantric practices is to have sex for twenty-four hours straight during a full moon with a woman who is having her period, and another is for a man to make love for many hours and withhold ejaculation. But some of the sexual practices that have tantric roots are very erotic and can help you appreciate the part of your relationship that is sacred.

Here are a few short tantric exercises. If you want more information, watch the *Playboy* video or read one of these excellent books: *The Art of Sexual Ecstasy* and *The Art of Sexual Magic* by Margo Anand or *Sexual Energy Ecstasy* by David and Ellen Ramsdale. There are also a number of workshops through organizations like The Learning Annex for those who would like specific training in tantra.

♀ Exercise ♂
Chakra Massage

The chakras are centers or vortexes where various types of energies— physical, emotional, mental, and electromagnetic—are exchanged or connected with the world around us. Traditionally, there are seven chakras, which run along the spine and up to the head, reflecting the development of human consciousness. They are located at the base of the spine (the "root center"), pelvis, navel or solar plexus, heart, throat, forehead (or "third eye"), and the crown of the head.

To release energy from these centers for sexual healing, do sensate focus caresses that start at the head chakras and move down to the pelvis to concentrate energy there. Concentrate on getting in touch with and feeling this energy.

♀ Exercise ♂
Tantric Intercourse

In tantric teaching there is a tremendous store of psychic energy that is locked or dormant in the root center at the base of the spine. Tantrics describe it as a coiled serpent, named Kundalini. When you become sexually aroused, this kundalini energy starts to uncoil and slowly move up your spinal chord, energizing the other centers as it goes. You may experience this as a white hot light moving along your spine or as actual sensations of muscular flexing and movement.

To awaken kundalini energy as you make love you should be in a straight back position, that is sitting or standing with your spine straight. Try the position with your partner, then the next time you make love switch positions so your partner can experience this. Make sure you come together in a grounding embrace (see the next exercise) after any tantric intercourse.

Raising kundalini energy can be a profound and beautiful experience. It can also make you disoriented and anxious. If it is something you decide to attempt more than occasionally, find a guide or instructor for this essentially spiritual practice.

♀ Exercise ♂
Grounding Embrace

After any tantric exercise or tantric intercourse, it is very important to re-center yourselves, or "get grounded." After you have profound or ecstatic sex, you will not feel like having a cigarette, taking a shower, or rolling over and going to sleep. You may feel wide-awake and vulnerable, and you probably will not feel like talking.

A good grounding exercise to do after tantric experiences is a version of the Eye Gaze bonding exercise in Chapter 3: lie quietly together face-to-face, hugging and holding each other, and simply gaze into each other's eyes. Let your breathing slow down naturally, let your energy naturally dissipate, and feel your hearts beat.

This is a lovely finish to the whole ecstatic experience. You will find that as your breathing and heart rates slow, they fall into sync with each other.

Ecstasy

As you and your partner may have already discovered while doing the sexual healing exercises, there is a level of sexual experience beyond arousal, and even beyond mutuality or intimacy. This is ecstasy. Sexual ecstasy is the feeling during a sexual encounter that you and your partner are so close that you temporarily transcend the material, physical plane of existence and enter into a highly spiritual realm as you have intercourse and orgasm together.

The way to find ecstasy together is to find balance between the male and female parts of yourselves. Ultimately, a woman is sexually healed by a man worshipping her body, especially her vagina or "sacred space." Since a major aspect of a woman's sexual strength is to contain semen and give birth, the way she reaches sexual ecstasy is to expel energy by releasing it in a series of explosive orgasms.

A man is healed by a woman's loving acceptance of his penis, his "wand of light," and by opening his heart. Since one aspect of man's sexual strength is his ability to ejaculate, he reaches sexual ecstasy by learning to contain that energy in order to have multiple orgasms.

A couple will be healed together by learning to transmit love and respect to each other through their genitals. You will accomplish this by your presence with each other and with your healing intentions.

The exercises in this book lay the foundation for the healing mindset necessary to understand and open the door to ecstasy. Spiritual experiences are always unique and highly personal, so I won't attempt describe a typical ecstatic moment. Some people say they see intense colors or images, some have visions, others hear music, and some feel an overwhelming sense of connection with all creation. You now have all the tools to use your loving connection as a gateway to the spiritual part of yourself and to connect with the spiritual soul of your partner.

The following two exercises are ways that lead to the planes of sexual ecstasy.

♀ Exercise ♂
Intercourse Exchanging Breath

Let's have the man active first. After he has done some sensual caresses with his partner, he kneels between his partner's legs and begins intercourse. As he continues to slowly and sensuously thrust, he leans over his partner and breathes into her mouth. They both visualize the breath flowing into her lungs, abdomen, and pelvis, and back into him through her vagina, and up his spine. This creates a sensational energy circle that you both can feel.

When the woman is active, she caresses her partner and, when he has a partial or full erection, she climbs on top. As she slowly and sensuously begins to thrust, she breathes into his mouth and they both visualize that the healing breath is flowing into his lungs, abdomen, pelvis, through his penis back into her and up her spine. The breath is a golden light that fills them both till they feel it radiating out of them.

This can be a very intense exercise. End by lying in a close, grounding embrace till both of you are ready to release your touch.

♀ Exercise ♂
Eye Gaze Intercourse

In this exercise you use your gaze to seduce your partner as you make love. This is seduction in a positive, beneficent sense. By gazing intently at your partner, you hypnotically draw your partner in and seduce him or her with your focus. As a surrogate, I sometimes did this with clients if they had a particularly difficult time focusing. I felt like Svengali.

Caress your partner as you both keep your eyes open and locked onto each other. Gaze deeply into his or her eyes as you climb on top and start to move, stroking up and down, in and out. Draw your sexual energies together as they build. Keep your movements sensuous and force your partner to look back at you with the power of the sexual energy you create.

After you come down from orgasm, lie together in a grounding embrace.

———

You are two people out there. Your pair bond is important. But it is also important to take the energy you have created and share that vitality with the world. As you embark on the journey of sexual healing, let the energies of your health and happiness spread to others, let the light of your sexual union add its healing magic to the good love out there in the world.

A Note from the Author

Although this book has been written with committed couples in mind, I believe anyone of any age or relationship history can experience some form of sexual healing. You have read this book because you are interested in experiencing this healing power. But the best approach for you and your particular problems may lie somewhere else.

There are many great books, lectures, and seminars out there on holistic health, covering topics like spontaneous remission, prayer, biofeedback, massage, relaxation, visualization, and other forms of alternative medicine. Over the years that I have taught sexual healing, I have found my approach to be completely consistent and compatible with other forms of alternative medicine. If you are already in a healing program of some sort, sexual healing can be a powerful addition to that program.

It is clear that lovemaking can benefit your health in general and specific ways. What about longevity? Will sexual healing prolong your life? Do people who make love rather than have sex live longer or have better or happier lives? We don't know, because no one has ever asked these questions before.

However, if you have a story to tell about your sexual healing experience, I would love to hear it, and I answer every letter. I am especially interested in hearing from couples who have used the exercises in Chapter 9 to heal their physical problems through lovemaking. If you have a sexual healing experience you would like to share, or if you have a question, please write to me in care of Hunter House Publishers, P.O. Box 2914, Alameda, CA 94501-0914.

Remember, touch heals, intimacy heals, and the loving sexual bond between two people in a mutual committed relationship is the most healing of all.

References

The Art of Sexual Ecstasy: The Path of the Sacred Sexuality for Western Lovers. Margo Anand. Los Angeles: Jeremy P. Tarcher, Inc., 1989. A beginning book for couples on tantric lovemaking and how sex can be a spiritual experience.

The Art of Sexual Magic. Margo Anand. New York: G.P. Putnam's Sons, 1995. An advanced book on tantric lovemaking; especially strong on creating erotic and spiritual couple rituals.

Bioenergetics. Alexander Lowen. New York: Penguin Books, 1975. Practical exercises to release psychic conflicts by changing body movements and postures.

Character Analysis. Wilhelm Reich. New York: Farrar, Strauss, and Giroux, 1945. Psychological theory that provides the basis for bioenergetics.

The Healing Power of Sex. J. Sachs. Englewood Cliffs, NJ: Prentice Hall, 1994. How sex and health are related; including discussions of how to have healthy sex, the difference between sex and sexuality, and the importance of self-image.

How to Make Love All Night. Barbara Keesling. New York: HarperCollins, 1994. How men can become multiply orgasmic and how they can be more in tune with a woman's rhythms.

A Healing Intimacy. Paul Pearsall. New York: Crown Books, 1995. Describes Dr. Pearsall's healing from cancer, which he attributes to his intimate relationship with his wife. Includes discussions of personality factors and lovemaking in healing.

Living the Therapeutic Touch. Dolores Krieger, R.N. New York: Dodd, Mead and Company, 1987.

Excellent summaries of research on touch in medical settings, originally written for nurses to help patients regain health faster.

Opening Up. James Pennebaker. New York: Morrow, 1990.
Very powerful, practical exercises on how to heal yourself from
trauma using self-disclosure, both talking and writing.

The Relaxation Response. Herbert Benson. New York: Anchor
Books, 1975.
The classic book explaining both the theory and practice of learning to
trigger the parasympathetic nervous system's relaxation ability.

The Self-Healing Personality. H.S. Friedman. New York: Henry
Holt, 1991.
The personality factors in why some people get sick while others
stay well. Also includes a good basic description of immune system
and how it works.

*Sexual Pleasure: Reaching New Heights of Sexual Arousal and Inti-
macy.* Barbara Keesling. Alameda, CA: Hunter House, 1993.
A sensate-focus program, with separate exercises for women and
men, and for couples to do together.

Spontaneous Healing. Andrew Weil. New York: Alfred A.
Knopf, Inc, 1995.
How to change your health habits to give yourself the best chance
of healing from illness and serious illnesses.

Talk Sexy to the One You Love. Barbara Keesling. New York:
HarperCollins, 1996.
How to verbally seduce your partner, how to communicate about
lovemaking, and how to give yourself permission to learn about
your sexual body.

Touching: The Human Significance of the Skin. Ashley Montagu.
New York: Harper & Row, Publishers, 1986, 3rd ed.
The classic book on touch research; covers research with animals and
human beings, psychology, sociology, anthropology, and medicine.

About the Photographers

Paul Dahlquist enjoys the art of photography as a means of celebrating what really is. He is now living in Portland, Oregon.

Michael Gesinger lives and works just outside of Seattle, Washington. He has been a fine art photographer for more than twenty years. His work has been exhibited in galleries and museums throughout the country.

Craig Morey is the author of two monographs, Studio Nudes (1992) and Body/Expression/Silence (1994). His photographs have appeared in such magazines as *Penthouse, Libido, La Fotografia,* and *The Journal of Erotica*, and have also been widely published in Europe, Asia, and the United States.

Charlotte Morrison is a photographer who lives in Capitola, California. Her work deals primarily with figure studies of the nude.

Ralph Steinmeier, a fashion photographer for twelve years, now specializes in photographing women solo and with their lovers. The black-and-white photos are shadowed and softened to make them artistic and mysterious. Steinmeier has been on HBO's *Real Sex* and the Playboy Channel. His erotic work has appeared in *Libido* and *Cupido* magazines.

Index